Ginny Jackson

MAy The Love of
God and His Sweet
Presence embrace
you everyday

Blessings
Anusha Moodley
Logos Hope 2018

GRACE

GRACE

Randy Alcorn

HARVEST HOUSE PUBLISHERS
EUGENE, OREGON

Cover by Harvest House Publishers

Cover photos © Igor Ovsyannykov, Liane Metzler / Unsplash

Back cover author photo © Angie Hunt

GRACE

Copyright © 2016 by Randy Alcorn
Published by Harvest House Publishers
Eugene, Oregon 97402
www.harvesthousepublishers.com

ISBN 978-0-7369-6746-4 (pbk.)

Printed in China

16 17 18 19 20 21 22 23 24 / RDS-JC / 10 9 8 7 6 5 4 3 2 1

"Grace comes into the soul,
as the morning sun into the world;
first a dawning, then a light;
and at last the sun in his full and
excellent brightness."
Thomas Adams

To Kathy Norquist and Chelsea Weber,
the finest assistants anyone could ask for!

Your devotion to Christ, love for people, and loyalty and ministry skills have been extraordinary.

Kath, for decades at church and at EPM, you've served with uncommon grace, wisdom, kindness, and patience. Your and Ron's friendship with our family has been a treasure. I'm so glad you're continuing with EPM in your new role!

Chels, ever since you took over as my assistant, you've been exceptional. Your contribution to our wonderful EPM staff has been terrific. I love your heart, initiative, attention to detail, and thirst for theological insight. (And your tiny house is cool too!)

Nanci and I thank God for how you both have gone above and beyond the call of duty and made our lives easier.

I don't deserve what you've done and still do for me. And since grace, both God's and yours, is undeserved, it's fitting to dedicate this book to you.

INTRODUCTION
Grace:
Beautiful and Scandalous

Grace is a delightful word.

People in hundreds of languages sing "Amazing Grace." Agnostics, skeptics, and hardened criminals have shed tears upon hearing the song.

Nothing is as stunning or as hope-giving as God's grace. And nothing more glorious. Jonathan Edwards wrote, "Grace is but Glory begun, and Glory is but Grace perfected."

But grace also confounds and even offends our human pride and independence. (How *dare* anyone suggest I don't deserve grace—and how dare they show grace to those I *know* don't deserve it?)

During a British conference on comparative religions, scholars debated what belief, if any, was unique to the Christian faith. Incarnation? Resurrection? The debate went on until C.S. Lewis wandered into the room.

"That's easy," Lewis replied. "It's grace."

Our pride insists we must work our way to God. Only the Christian faith presents God's grace as unconditional. Other religions insist we must do good to earn God's favor—and if we stop, we lose it.

But the Bible shows we're unworthy of God's grace and can't earn it. What we cannot earn we cannot lose. We can't *stop deserving* his grace since we never deserved it in the first place.

The Bible makes this astounding proclamation: "God demonstrates his own love for us in this: While we were still sinners, Christ died for us" (Romans 5:8).

Jesus, the sinless one, willingly gave himself over to be tortured—not for anything he had done, but to save those least deserving. We were not merely misguided subjects; we were rebels and traitors against the King. Yet God adopts us as his children and happily gives us a seat at his table.

If this seems less than amazing, less than wonderful, then we really don't grasp the meaning of grace.

Some people worry that because they've failed God so often, they're unworthy of his grace. But it's that very unworthiness that motivated John Newton, the English slave trader whom God wondrously converted, to compose the classic hymn. And because every Christian heart is touched by grace, "Amazing Grace" still moves us to heartfelt gratitude today.

Charles Spurgeon said something profound and still timely:

> Don't buy the lie that cultivating condemnation and wallowing in your shame is somehow

pleasing to God, or that a constant, low-grade guilt will somehow promote holiness and spiritual maturity. It's just the opposite! God is glorified when we believe with all our hearts that those who trust in Christ can never be condemned. It's only when we receive his free gift of grace and live in the good of total forgiveness that we're able to turn from old, sinful ways of living and walk in grace-motivated obedience.

Spurgeon is one of many "dead people" (now alive in Christ's presence) that I quote in this book, because insights about grace came long ago in church history, and we need to hear these proven voices from the past who often have far more to offer us than our contemporaries do.

I hope you'll spend time meditating on the brief reflections, great quotations, and Scriptures in this book. God promises that his Word "will not return to me empty, but will accomplish what I desire and achieve the purpose for which I sent it" (Isaiah 55:11).

As you read and contemplate and share these insights with others (highly recommended), may you draw closer to Jesus, and may he flood you with gratitude for his magnificent and delightful grace!

Randy Alcorn

DAY 1

*I do not set aside the grace of God, for if
righteousness could be gained through
the law, Christ died for nothing!*

GALATIANS 2:21

Grace never ignores the awful reality of our sin. In fact, it emphasizes it. Paul said if men were good enough, then "Christ died for nothing." Benjamin Warfield said, "Grace is free sovereign favor to the ill-deserving." If we don't see the reality of how ill-deserving we are, God's grace won't seem amazing. If we minimize our unworthiness, we minimize God's grace.

"Amazing grace—how sweet the sound—
That saved a wretch like me!
I once was lost but now am found,
Was blind but now I see."

John Newton

DAY 2

For the message of the cross is foolishness to those who are perishing, but to us who are being saved it is the power of God.

1 Corinthians 1:18

A.W. Tozer said, "Grace is the good pleasure of God that inclines him to bestow benefits upon the undeserving...to save us and make us sit together in heavenly places to demonstrate to the ages the exceeding riches of God's kindness to us in Christ Jesus."

The problem of how to reconcile evil people with a God who hates evil is the greatest problem of history. It calls for the greatest solution ever devised, one so radical as to be nearly unthinkable, and to offend the sensibilities of countless people throughout history—the cross.

> "The ultimate test of our spirituality is the measure of our amazement at the grace of God."
>
> **Martyn Lloyd-Jones**

DAY 3

God, have mercy on me, a sinner.

LUKE 18:13

Sinclair Ferguson says, "The spiritual life is lived between two polarities: our sin and God's grace. The discovery of the former brings us to seek the latter; the work of the latter illuminates the depths of the former and causes us to seek yet more grace."

Let's face each day and each person we see with humility, as an act of grace, while reminding ourselves that we too desperately need God's grace—every bit as much as those we're offering it to. When we're acutely aware of our own sins, we'll proclaim and exemplify God's "good news of happiness" (Isaiah 52:7 ESV), not with a spirit of superiority but with the contagious excitement of one hungry person sharing food with another.

> "God's grace is his active favor bestowing the greatest gift upon those who have deserved the greatest punishment."
>
> William Hendrickson

DAY 4

*Let us then approach God's throne of grace
with confidence, so that we may receive mercy
and find grace to help us in our time of need.*

Hebrews 4:16

To a devout Jew, the notion of unhindered access to God
was scandalous. Yet *by* his grace and *for* his grace, that access
is ours. Because of Christ's work, God's door is always open
to us. Let's enter freely and frequently!

"Now I will say this to every sinner, though he
should think himself to be the worst sinner
who ever lived: cry to the Lord and seek him
while he may be found. By simple faith, go
to your Savior, for he is the throne of grace."

Charles Spurgeon

DAY 5

*The Lord, the Lord, the compassionate and
gracious God, slow to anger, abounding in love
and faithfulness, maintaining love to thousands,
and forgiving wickedness, rebellion and sin.*

Exodus 34:6-7

There's little consolation in knowing God is your Creator unless you know what he's like. A Creator could be miserable, unreasonable, unloving, and downright hateful. Likewise, there is little consolation in knowing God is your Ruler, but great consolation in knowing that God is your sovereign Savior: holy, happy, kind, and full of grace.

> "Nothing can alter the character of God. In the course of a human life, tastes and outlook and temper may change radically: a kind, equable man may turn bitter and crotchety; a man of good-will may grow cynical and callous. But nothing of this sort happens to the Creator. He never becomes less truthful, or merciful, or just, or good, than he used to be."
>
> J.I. Packer

DAY 6

From his abundance we have all received
one gracious blessing after another.

John 1:16 (nlt)

Robert Murray M'Cheyne said, "If grace were at any time an obligation of God, it would cease to be grace."

Deliberately and unceasingly, the tide of God's grace brings us wave after wave of God's goodness. The next wave crashes onto the beach before the previous wave is diminished. God's grace is constant, but it isn't stationary. It keeps moving toward us day by day, hour by hour, minute by minute. It's always there when we need it—and there's never a moment we don't.

Conviction of sin brings us momentary grief. Yet, as Sinclair Ferguson says, "The heart-conviction of sin is the way grace prepares the heart for more grace."

> "Between here and heaven, every minute that
> the Christian lives will be a minute of grace."
>
> Charles Spurgeon

DAY 7

Yet he gave a command to the skies above
and opened the doors of the heavens;
he rained down manna for the people to eat,
he gave them the grain of heaven.

PSALM 78:23-24

Louis Cassels wrote, "If God wants you to do something, he'll make it possible for you to do it, but the grace he provides comes only with the task and cannot be stockpiled beforehand. We are dependent on him from hour to hour."

As God didn't allow the Israelites to store up manna, he doesn't let us store up grace. He always gives us enough, but we can't deposit it for the future. We have to get it fresh, every day.

"He giveth more grace
when the burdens grow greater,
He sendeth more strength
when the labors increase;
To added affliction he addeth His mercy,
To multiplied trials His multiplied peace."

Annie Johnson Flint

DAY 8

I am not ashamed of the gospel, because it is the
power of God that brings salvation to everyone
who believes... "The righteous will live by faith."

ROMANS 1:16-17

The grace that saves us is also the grace that sanctifies and empowers us. God's power isn't needed just by unbelievers to be converted. It's needed by believers to be obedient and joyful. Jerry Bridges puts it, "The grace that saves the sinner is the power that must supply the sinner."

We can look back at the day we first experienced the sunrise of God's grace. But grace is a sun that never sets in the believer's life.

John Calvin said, "Grace does not grant permission to live in the flesh; it supplies power to live in the Spirit."

> "One thing is past all question: we shall bring our
> Lord most glory if we get from him much grace."
>
> **Charles Spurgeon**

DAY 9

*Here is a trustworthy saying that deserves full
acceptance: Christ Jesus came into the world
to save sinners—of whom I am the worst.*

1 TIMOTHY 1:15

Harry Ironside wrote, "Grace is the very opposite of merit...Grace is not only undeserved favor, but it is favor shown to the one who has deserved the very opposite."

It should shock us that Jesus went to Hell on the cross so we'll never get what we deserve. We've grown too accustomed to grace—we need to be astounded by it. God promises nothing will ever separate us from his love (Romans 8:38-39). Incredible...but it's a blood-bought promise we can count on.

> "Love is not the upward ascent of our souls
> that sublimates us into union with the deity.
> Rather, love is the descent of God's royal
> grace that conquers our rebellion, atones
> for our guilt, and draws us into sonship."
>
> **Edmund P. Clowney**

DAY 10

*In him we have redemption through his blood,
the forgiveness of sins, in accordance with the
riches of God's grace that he lavished on us.*

Ephesians 1:7

Benjamin Jowett said, "Grace is the energy of the divine affection rolling in plenteousness toward the shores of human need."

No matter what you've done, there is no sin beyond the reach of God's grace once you have accepted Christ's offer of forgiveness. Max Lucado says, "God answers the mess of life with one word: grace!"

God knows everything, so no sin surprises him. He knows all our worst secrets (Psalm 69:5). No skeletons will ever fall out of our closets. Jesus will never say, "Had I known you'd done that, I'd never have let you into Heaven." He's seen us at our worst and still loves us.

> "Are you too bad to receive grace? How could you be too bad to receive what is for the bad?"
>
> David Powlison

DAY 11

Christ Jesus came into the world to save sinners—
of whom I am the worst. But for that very
reason I was shown mercy so that in me, the
worst of sinners, Christ Jesus might display his
immense patience as an example for those who
would believe in him and receive eternal life.

1 TIMOTHY 1:15-16

The apostle Paul not only approved of Stephen's murder (Acts 22:20), he "began to destroy the church. Going from house to house, he dragged off both men and women and put them in prison" (Acts 8:3). He called himself the worst of sinners. Yet God forgave him, even elevating him to leadership in the church. There are no limits to the forgiving grace of God. Christ chose Paul for both redemption and service; he has done the same for us.

"The cross was an act simultaneously
of punishment and amnesty, severity
and grace, justice and mercy."

John Stott

DAY 12

*The grace of God has appeared that
offers salvation to all people.*

Titus 2:11

W.A. Elwell wrote, "No other system of religious thought, past or present, contains an emphasis on divine grace comparable to that of the Bible."

But just as words such as *love* and *happiness* are often misused and misunderstood, so too is *grace*.

Tolerance is the world's substitute for grace. This fake grace of indifference negates or trivializes incarnation, redemption, and the need for regeneration. True grace recognizes and deals with sin in the most radical and painful way: Christ's redemption. God in his grace offers salvation to all people because *all people need his salvation.* Christ came precisely because not one of us is fine without him.

"He drank a cup of wrath without mercy that
we might drink a cup of mercy without wrath."

J. Oswald Sanders

DAY 13

*The next day John saw Jesus coming toward
him and said, "Look, the Lamb of God,
who takes away the sin of the world!"*

JOHN 1:29

Jesus was and is Grace and Truth fully embodied (John 1:14). Not half-grace and half-truth, but full grace and full truth.

When Jesus saves us, we become new creatures in him (2 Corinthians 5:17). We start seeing sin for what it really is—bondage, not freedom.

Thomas Brooks said, "Saving grace makes a man as willing to leave his lusts as a slave is willing to leave his galley, or a prisoner his dungeon, or a thief his bolts, or a beggar his rags."

> "No man shall ever behold the glory of Christ by sight in heaven who does not, in some measure, behold it by faith in this world. Grace is a necessary preparation for glory and faith for sight."
>
> **John Owen**

DAY 14

*To him who is able to keep you from stumbling
and to present you before his glorious presence
without fault and with great joy—to the
only God our Savior be glory, majesty, power
and authority, through Jesus Christ our Lord,
before all ages, now and forevermore! Amen.*

JUDE 24-25

God's grace didn't get us started then leave us to our works. Grace sustains us in the present and will deliver us in the future. Trevin Wax says, "Whatever you attempt to supplement grace with is what you will eventually supplant grace with."

Paul said, "How foolish can you be? After starting your new lives in the Spirit, why are you now trying to become perfect by your own human effort?" (Galatians 3:3 NLT).

"Through many dangers, toils and snares
I have already come;
'Tis grace hath brought me safe thus far,
And grace will lead me home."

John Newton

DAY 15

The law was given through Moses;
grace and truth came through Jesus Christ.

JOHN 1:17

Martin Luther said, "Christ is no Moses, no exactor, no giver of laws, but a giver of grace, a Savior; he is infinite mercy and goodness, freely and bountifully given to us."

As God gives us grace, we are to show grace to others, a grace infused with truth. Real grace is never extended in disregard of truth. Birds need two wings to fly. With only one wing, they're grounded. The gospel flies with the wings of grace and truth. Not one, but both.

> "Truth without love is harshness; it gives us information but in such a way that we cannot really hear it. Love without truth is sentimentality; it supports and affirms us but keeps us in denial about our flaws."
>
> Timothy Keller

DAY 16

Since you excel in so many ways...I want you to excel also in this gracious act of giving.

2 Corinthians 8:7 (nlt)

Life without grace is profoundly unhappy. At the beginning of *A Christmas Carol,* Ebenezer Scrooge is wealthy but miserable. Self-centered people fail to extend grace by giving to others. No wonder—they've never received God's grace themselves.

Second Corinthians 8–9, the longest biblical passage on giving, is full of references to grace. After Scrooge's transformation, he walks the London streets, freely distributing his wealth to the needy. He's giddy with delight. Grace will do that to you!

> "Some people laughed to see the alteration in [Scrooge], but he let them laugh, and little heeded them...His own heart laughed, and that was quite enough for him. And it was always said of him, that he knew how to keep Christmas well, if any man alive possessed the knowledge."

> Charles Dickens

DAY 17

*Come, all you who are thirsty,
come to the waters;
and you who have no money,
come, buy and eat!
Come, buy wine and milk
without money and without cost.*

Isaiah 55:1

There's only one requirement for enjoying God's grace: being broke...and knowing it. That's why Jesus said, "Happy are those who know they are spiritually poor; the Kingdom of heaven belongs to them!" (Matthew 5:3 GNT).

God promises his children that our lives don't end here: we never pass our peaks, we need no bucket lists, and our future life will be forever better than this one. David Jeremiah says, "The sense of lost opportunity is rooted in a faulty understanding of God's grace. Likewise, when grace is grasped and embraced, the Land of Opportunity becomes yours again."

> "The cost for the recipient of God's grace
> is nothing—and no price could be
> higher for arrogant people to pay."
>
> **Dan Allender**

DAY 18

All of us have become like one who is unclean,
and all our righteous acts are like filthy rags;
we all shrivel up like a leaf,
and like the wind our sins sweep us away.

ISAIAH 64:6

For some, "human depravity" (total inability to earn our way to God) may be an insulting doctrine, but grasping it is liberating. When I realize the best I can do without God is like "filthy rags" in his sight, it finally sinks in that I have nothing to offer. Salvation therefore hinges on his work, not mine. What a relief!

> "We could not take one step in the pursuit of holiness if God in his grace had not first delivered us from the dominion of sin and brought us into union with his risen Son. Salvation is by grace and sanctification is by grace."
>
> **Jerry Bridges**

DAY 19

There before me was a throne in heaven
with someone sitting on it...
Around the throne were four living creatures...
Day and night they never stop saying,
"Holy, holy, holy is the Lord God Almighty,
who was, and is, and is to come."

REVELATION 4:2,6,8

Hope is the light at the end of life's tunnel. It not only makes the tunnel endurable, it fills the heart with anticipation. Not just of a better world, but by God's grace a new and perfect world. A world alive, fresh, beautiful, devoid of pain, suffering, and war, a world without earthquakes, without tsunamis, without tragedy. A world ruled by the only One worthy of ruling.

"The law works fear and wrath;
grace works hope and mercy."

Martin Luther

DAY 20

*Just as through the disobedience of the
one man the many were made sinners, so
also through the obedience of the one man
the many will be made righteous.*

ROMANS 5:19

God's children *have been saved* from the penalty of sin, we
are being saved from the power of sin, and we *will be saved*
from the presence of sin. Salvation, sanctification, and glo-
rification are all grounded solidly in exactly the same thing:
God's grace.

The grace of Jesus isn't an add-on or makeover that
enhances our lives. It causes a radical transformation—
from being sin-enslaved to being righteousness-liberated.
Religions can alter behavior. Only Jesus has the power to
transform the heart. The work of Christ provides the only
foundation on which we can build a new life.

"There is a danger that grace can become a topic
we discuss rather than a power we experience."

Heath Lambert

DAY 21

Through him we have also obtained access by faith into this grace in which we stand, and we rejoice in hope of the glory of God. Not only that, but we rejoice in our sufferings, knowing that suffering produces endurance, and endurance produces character, and character produces hope.

ROMANS 5:2-4 (ESV)

What if many of our most painful ordeals look quite different in a million years, as we recall them on the New Earth? What if one day we discover that, by his grace, God has wasted nothing in our life on Earth? What if we see at last that every agony was part of giving birth to an eternal joy?

"No man can estimate what is really happening at the present...Evil labors with vast power and perpetual success—in vain; preparing always only the soil for unexpected good to sprout in."

J.R.R. Tolkien

DAY 22

*He saved us, not because of righteous things
we had done, but because of his mercy.*

Titus 3:5

We're forever secure in Christ's love, as we could never be if our relationship with him depended upon our worth. He says of his sheep, "I give them eternal life, and they shall never perish; no one will snatch them out of my hand" (John 10:28).

John Newton said, "I am not what I might be, I am not what I ought to be, I am not what I wish to be, I am not what I hope to be. But I thank God I am not what I once was, and I can say with the great apostle, 'By the grace of God I am what I am.'"

> "When Christ is my hope, he becomes the
> one thing in which I have confidence. I act
> on his wisdom and bank on his grace."
>
> Paul Tripp

DAY 23

The law was brought in so that the trespass might increase. But where sin increased, grace increased all the more, so that, just as sin reigned in death, so also grace might reign through righteousness to bring eternal life through Jesus Christ our Lord.

ROMANS 5:20-21

Don't ever tell yourself you may as well go ahead and sin since God will forgive you. This cheapens grace. Grace that makes sin seem trivial is not true grace. God forgives when we sincerely repent. We prove that sincerity by taking necessary steps to avoid temptation. No sin is small that crucified Christ. Sin matters, yet grace overpowers sin, offering both forgiveness and transformed living. Every sin pales in comparison to God's grace to us in Christ.

> "Grace is not simply leniency when we have sinned. Grace is the enabling gift of God not to sin. Grace is power, not just pardon."
>
> **John Piper**

DAY 24

Then he took a cup, and when he had given thanks, he gave it to them, saying... "This is my blood of the covenant, which is poured out for many for the forgiveness of sins."

MATTHEW 26:27-28

No one deserves forgiveness. That's the point of grace. On the cross, Jesus experienced the Hell we deserve, so for all eternity we can experience the Heaven we don't deserve. The grace that is free for us is costly for God. But he offers it to us with a heart of infinite love.

> "I have come to know a God who has a soft spot for rebels, who recruits people like the adulterer David, the whiner Jeremiah, the traitor Peter, and the human-rights abuser Saul of Tarsus. I have come to know a God whose Son made prodigals...the trophies of his ministry."
>
> **Philip Yancey**

DAY 25

*The Word became flesh and made his dwelling
among us. We have seen his glory, the glory
of the one and only Son, who came from
the Father, full of grace and truth.*

JOHN 1:14

The greatest kindness we can offer each other is the truth. Our job isn't just to help each other *feel* good but to help each other *be* good.

Some imagine our options are to: (1) speak truth harshly; or (2) say nothing in the name of grace. Wrong. Jesus came full of grace *and* truth. We shouldn't choose between them, but act according to grace and truth.

Greg Laurie reminds us, "There is a built-in offense to the essential message of the gospel, but we don't have to make it worse by being insensitive to people."

> "A man who loves you the most is the man
> who tells you the most truth about yourself."
>
> **Robert Murray M'Cheyne**

DAY 26

God demonstrates his own love for us in this:
While we were still sinners, Christ died for us.

ROMANS 5:8

It's sometimes said, "Grace is God giving us what we do not deserve and mercy is God not giving us what we do deserve."

People often reason, "But I don't deserve forgiveness after all I've done." That's exactly right. None of us deserves forgiveness. If we deserved it, we wouldn't need it.

That's the whole point of grace. On the cross Christ received what we deserved so we could receive what we don't deserve—forgiveness, a clean slate, a fresh start, and an eternal life of unbridled happiness.

> "Your worst days are never so bad that you
> are beyond the reach of God's grace. And
> your best days are never so good that you
> are beyond the need of God's grace."
>
> **Jerry Bridges**

DAY 27

*Now Stephen, a man full of God's grace
and power, performed great wonders
and signs among the people.*

Acts 6:8

We should never believe anything about ourselves or God that makes his grace to us seem anything less than astonishing. Charles Hodge said, "The doctrines of grace humble a man without degrading him and exalt a man without inflating him."

Jonathan Edwards wrote, "There is a difference between having an opinion that God is...gracious, and having a sense of the loveliness and beauty of that...grace. There is a difference between having a rational judgment that honey is sweet, and having a sense of its sweetness."

May we taste daily the sweetness of God's grace!

> "Unfathomable oceans of grace are in Christ
> for you. Dive and dive again, you will never
> come to the bottom of these depths."
>
> **Robert Murray M'Cheyne**

DAY 28

This is love: not that we loved God, but that he loved us and sent his Son as an atoning sacrifice for our sins.

1 John 4:10

Steven Lawson says, "Salvation is not a reward for the righteous, but a gift for the guilty."

Grace isn't about God lowering his standards, but fulfilling those standards through Christ's substitutionary atonement.

Gary Edmonds says of relief work, "If we bring aid without bringing a Savior, we have not brought enough!" (Let's bring all the relief we can...and the gospel with it.)

We don't need just a little help from our Savior here and there. We need an immense amount here and now.

> "Men may flee from the sunlight to dark and musty caves of the earth, but they cannot put out the sun. So men may in any dispensation despise the grace of God, but they cannot extinguish it."
>
> A.W. Tozer

DAY 29

He will wipe every tear from their eyes. There will be no more death or mourning or crying or pain, for the old order of things has passed away.

REVELATION 21:4

While God will wipe away the tears and sorrow attached to this world, the drama of God's work in human history will not be erased from our minds. Heaven's happiness will not hinge on our ignorance of what happened on Earth. Rather, it will be greatly enhanced by our informed appreciation of God's glorious grace and justice throughout Earth's history—including in the many things that made no sense to us.

"Earth has no sorrow that Heaven cannot heal."

Thomas More

DAY 30

*God raised us up with Christ and seated us
with him in the heavenly realms in Christ
Jesus, in order that in the coming ages he might
show the incomparable riches of his grace,
expressed in his kindness to us in Christ Jesus.*

EPHESIANS 2:6-7

After we die we'll forever be learning about and experiencing God's grace toward us. We'll likely look back at our lives in this fallen world and see the riches of God's grace and kindness to us, though our hardships may have seemed anything but grace-filled and kind.

This will be the power of retrospect—seeing afterward that all God's promises were true all along. May God give us his grace not to wait until we die to discover this, but to believe his Word here and now.

> "The most stinging memories from our past can be powerful reminders of God's grace and forgiveness, living monuments of his mercy in our lives—markers that keep us dependent and trusting."

Nancy Leigh DeMoss

DAY 31

The LORD replied [to Jonah],
"Is it right for you to be angry?"

JONAH 4:4

Like the prodigal son's older brother, Jonah resented God's grace in withholding judgment against the city of Nineveh. But to resent God's grace to others is to spurn his grace to us. As the saying goes, "Resentment is like taking poison and waiting for the other person to die."

Because the doctrine of grace is so foreign to many, it may take time and patience to teach it. Spurgeon said, "If the people do not like the doctrine of grace, give them all the more of it." If there's one thing we desperately need, it's acquiring a taste for God's liberating grace.

> "God is in debt to no one. It's only out of
> his inexhaustible riches that he has given
> anything to anyone. 'Tis all of grace."
>
> Kevin DeYoung

DAY 32

Moreover, when God gives someone wealth
and possessions, and the ability to enjoy
them, to accept their lot and be happy
in their toil—this is a gift of God.

ECCLESIASTES 5:19

Sometimes people who are determined to avoid putting things ahead of God miss a thousand daily opportunities to thank him, praise him, and draw near to him because they imagine they shouldn't enjoy what God has made. But God is a lavish giver, and through his grace he "richly provides us with everything for our enjoyment" (1 Timothy 6:17).

We should learn to see God consciously in every gift he gives us. If we recognize they are from his hand, appreciating them is worshipping him.

"In despising the gifts, we insult the Giver."

John Calvin

DAY 33

*As for you, you were dead in your transgressions
and sins, in which you used to live when
you followed the ways of this world.*

Ephesians 2:1

You and I weren't merely sick in our sins; we were dead in
our sins. That means I'm not just unworthy of salvation;
I'm utterly incapable of earning it. Corpses can't raise themselves from the grave.

What a relief to realize that my salvation is completely
the result of God's grace. It cannot be earned by good
works—and therefore can't be lost by bad ones. Thomas
Watson wrote, "Acts of grace cannot be reversed. God blots
out his people's sins, but not their names."

> "If you and sin are friends, you and
> God are not yet reconciled."
>
> J.C. Ryle

DAY 34

The true light that gives light to everyone
was coming into the world.

JOHN 1:9

The very word *grace* is happy-making. P.J. Achtemeier writes that grace is "the English translation of a Greek word meaning concretely 'that which brings delight, joy, happiness, or good fortune.'"

That Jesus came as the light that "gives light to everyone" indicates all people have benefited from Christ's coming, even (for a time) those who reject him. The model of Christ, his grace and truth, his elevation of women and slaves, and his conciliatory words, have brought greater freedom and civil rights to many societies. But there's no substitute for his saving grace, since eternity hangs in the balance.

> "You will never find Jesus so precious as when the world is one vast howling wilderness. Then he is like a rose blooming in the midst of the desolation, a rock rising above the storm."
>
> **Robert Murray M'Cheyne**

DAY 35

*Do not set your heart on what you will
eat or drink; do not worry about it...
But seek his kingdom, and these things
will be given to you as well.*

Luke 12:29,31

When we come to Christ, God graciously puts all his resources at our disposal. He also expects us, as a glad response to grace, to put all our resources at his disposal. That's a dramatically uneven exchange since God has so much more than we do, and all we have comes from him in the first place.

> "I am no longer my own, but Yours. Put me to what You will, rank me with whom You will; put me to doing, put me to suffering; let me be employed for You or laid aside for You, exalted for You or brought low for You...I freely and wholeheartedly yield all things to Your pleasure and disposal."

John Wesley

DAY 36

You open your hand
and satisfy the desires of every living thing.

PSALM 145:16

It is characteristic of bad people to not *think* of themselves as bad. We imagine we're good (not perfect, but good enough). So we fail to marvel at God's common yet extraordinary grace. We never say, "Where is a just God? Why hasn't he struck me down for my sin today?" Instead, we moan that someone took our parking space.

> "An unthankful and complaining spirit is an abiding sin against God, and a cause of almost continual unhappiness; and yet how common such a spirit is. How prone we seem to be to forget the good that life knows, and remember and brood over its evil—to forget its joys, and think only of its sorrows—to forget thankfulness, and remember only to complain."
>
> John Broadus

DAY 37

Command those who are rich in this present
world not to be arrogant nor to put their
hope in wealth, which is so uncertain, but to
put their hope in God, who richly provides
us with everything for our enjoyment.

1 TIMOTHY 6:17

Why trust God when you think all your bases are covered? Why ask him for daily bread when you own the bakery? We pride ourselves on financial independence, but where would we be without the grace of God, who gives every breath as a gift?

Wealth insulates us from discerning the depth of our need—which is why Jesus said it's so hard for the rich to enter his kingdom (Matthew 19:23-24). Grace blazed the one trail by which every person may find God, and thereby Heaven.

> "Grace will devastate your selfish dreams
> while it secures for you an eternal future
> far better than your wildest dreams."
>
> Paul Tripp

DAY 38

He has rescued us from the dominion
of darkness and brought us into the
kingdom of the Son he loves.

COLOSSIANS 1:13

Grace is God's work to deliver us from the full extent of our depravity and the full extent of our punishment. A rescue is only as dramatic and consequential as the fate from which someone is rescued. By underestimating depravity and denying eternal Hell, Satan tries to lower redemption's price tag, cheapening the grace that paid the price. Mark Dever says, "Forgetfulness of God's grace is one of the greatest tools in the enemy's war against our souls."

"His love has no limit,
His grace has no measure,
His pow'r has no boundary known unto men;
For out of His infinite riches in Jesus
He giveth and giveth and giveth again."

Annie Johnson Flint

DAY 39

We all, who with unveiled faces contemplate the Lord's glory, are being transformed into his image with ever-increasing glory, which comes from the Lord, who is the Spirit.

2 CORINTHIANS 3:18

We each have our preferred ways of sinning, whether as porn addicts, materialists, gossips, or the self-righteous. We hate the idea of Hell precisely because we don't hate evil. We hate it also because we deserve it. And since grace reminds us we deserve Hell, it's possible to hate grace also. (Like the prodigal son's older brother did.)

We define our good in terms of what brings us health and pleasure now. But God in his grace defines it in terms of what makes us more like Jesus and gives us the deeper happiness of enjoying the pleasures at his right hand.

> "Hell is full of people who think they deserve heaven. Heaven is full of people who know they deserve hell."
>
> **Trevin Wax**

DAY 40

He has saved us and called us to a holy life—not because of anything we have done but because of his own purpose and grace. This grace was given us in Christ Jesus before the beginning of time.

2 TIMOTHY 1:9

How could God give us grace before the universe existed? God determined in advance Christ's work for us on the cross. God wrote the script of the unfolding drama of redemption long before we took the stage. The Bible's first three chapters set up the story; its last three show how God will judge evil, reward good, and descend to the New Earth to live with his children. He'll wipe away every tear from their eyes, guaranteeing no more suffering and evil. It's the greatest story ever told—and it's 100 percent true!

"Sometimes when we get overwhelmed
we forget how big God is."

A.W. Tozer

DAY 41

*His divine power has given us everything we need
for a godly life through our knowledge of him
who called us by his own glory and goodness.*

2 PETER 1:3

Richard Sibbes said, "By grace we are what we are in justification, and work what we work in sanctification."

God doesn't want us to live the Christian life by self-powered works and sin management. Rather, he calls us to acknowledge our spiritual impotence moment by moment, accepting his grace every hour, living in boundless gratitude and therefore unswerving joy.

God loves us so much that he grants his grace to change us. David Garland says, "God is in the business not of whitewashing sins but of transforming sinners." Grace is a superlative gift, and the proper response to it is overwhelming and overflowing gratitude.

"It is a sure mark of grace to desire more."

Robert Murray M'Cheyne

DAY 42

He was not far from the house when the centurion sent friends to say to him: "Lord, don't trouble yourself, for I do not deserve to have you come under my roof. That is why I did not even consider myself worthy to come to you."

Luke 7:6-7

When asked, "How are you doing?" a good response is, "Better than I deserve." We aren't worthy of redemption or God's multitude of graces, his thousands of daily gifts, big and small.

Not just on the best, but on the worst day of your life, God's grace is there for you. When we know we deserve eternal damnation, doesn't it put a "bad day" in perspective?

> "The doctrines of grace humble a man without degrading him and exalt a man without inflating him."
>
> Charles Hodge

DAY 43

*I say to you that many will come from
the east and the west, and will take their
places at the feast with Abraham, Isaac
and Jacob in the kingdom of heaven.*

Matthew 8:11

What will it be like to feast with God's people of all times and places? Imagine the wonder of it, the stories we will hear and tell! On God's New Earth, when we gather at meals and other times, we'll recite God's acts of grace throughout our lives. Some gracious acts we didn't understand, some we resented, and others we never caught sight of. We'll see then with an eternal perspective. But we don't need to wait until we die to trust God and celebrate his grace. Let's learn to do it today...right here and right now.

"Open your Bible. It is the pilgrim's guide, in which
God describes the glory yet to be revealed."

Charles Spurgeon

DAY 44

It is by grace you have been saved...
For we are God's handiwork,
created in Christ Jesus to do good works,
which God prepared in advance for us to do.

Ephesians 2:8,10

Though we're saved by grace and not works, Scripture tells us we're created to do specific works God has predetermined. Some Christians minimize the importance of works, not distinguishing between self-righteous works that can't earn salvation and Christ-empowered works after salvation that God in his grace rewards us for. We're never to work *for* but to work *out* our salvation with fear and trembling (Philippians 2:12). Don't miss the joy of doing for others what God prepared for you to do.

> "The distance between working out your salvation and working for your salvation is the distance between heaven and hell."

Matt Smethurst

DAY 45

O Lord, your unfailing love fills the earth;
teach me your decrees.

Psalm 119:64 (NLT)

William Bernard Ullanthorne wrote, "The burden of life is from ourselves, its lightness from the grace of Christ and the love of God." If we fail to see evidences of God's unfailing love and grace in our lives, it is not because they're lacking but because we're blind.

Difficulties are sure to come, but God has a sovereign and good purpose in them, and we are totally secure in Christ's unconditional and unfailing love. "Who shall separate us from the love of Christ?" (Romans 8:35). No one.

God, open our eyes to your daily goodness to us!

"Seek to cultivate a buoyant, joyous sense of the crowded kindnesses of God in your daily life."

Alexander Maclaren

DAY 46

If by grace, then it cannot be based on works;
if it were, grace would no longer be grace.

ROMANS 11:6

On the one hand, God's grace in our hearts can be expected to produce good works: "And God is able to make all grace abound to you, so that having all sufficiency in all things at all times, you may abound in every good work" (2 Corinthians 9:8 ESV). But our good works are the result, not the cause, of God's grace.

God's grace is one-sided. Human merit and divine grace cannot coexist in salvation. The gospel isn't something we do, it's something Christ did for us. It rests on the solid rock of God's faithfulness. Neither our failures nor our mortality can negate it.

"Grace finds us beggars but leaves us debtors."

Augustus Toplady

DAY 47

*Therefore, since we are surrounded by such
a great cloud of witnesses, let us throw off
everything that hinders and the sin that so easily
entangles. And let us run with perseverance
the race marked out for us, fixing our eyes on
Jesus, the pioneer and perfecter of faith. For
the joy set before him he endured the cross.*

HEBREWS 12:1-2

Godly living centers not on what we avoid but on whom
we embrace. Anytime we talk more about dos and don'ts
than about Jesus and his grace, something's wrong. Check-
off-the-box holiness that measures itself by sin avoidance
won't last. Finding superior happiness in Christ over any
and all sin is true Jesus-centered holiness. And it's infinitely
more satisfying than its imitations.

"He must be happy who is holy...*Sin* is the parent
of all misery; *holiness* the root of all happiness."

Octavius Winslow

DAY 48

That I may gain Christ and be found in him, not having a righteousness of my own that comes from the law, but that which is through faith in Christ—the righteousness that comes from God on the basis of faith.

PHILIPPIANS 3:8-9

The Christian life is grace-centered, making it far more than sin management. Behavior modification that's not empowered by God's heart-changing grace is self-righteous, as repugnant to God as the worst sins people gossip about.

If in the end you get the credit for your righteousness, then it's self-righteousness not Jesus-righteousness. And self-righteousness is insufficient to open Heaven's doors to you (2 Corinthians 5:21). Furthermore, it makes life and relationships hopeless, because self-generated righteousness is a lie.

> "The doctrine of grace and redemption keeps us from seeing any person or situation as hopeless."
>
> **Timothy Keller**

DAY 49

Oh, that we might know the LORD!
Let us press on to know him.
He will respond to us
as surely as the arrival of dawn
or the coming of rains in early spring.

HOSEA 6:3 (NLT)

As we grow older, let's not be content to sit in our rocking chairs, looking back at those days when we trusted and served God. On the contrary, let's trust and serve God with greater zeal. Let's pour ourselves into serving others for God's glory and in gratitude for his grace.

"Would you grow in grace? If you would, your way is plain. Ask of God more faith. Beg of him simply to impress divine things more deeply on your heart, to give you more and more of the substance of things hoped for and of the evidence of things not seen."

E.M. Bounds

DAY 50

*Many are the plans in a person's heart,
but it is the LORD's purpose that prevails.*

PROVERBS 19:21

May God give us all grace to trust that he sees the unseen and plans our lives with benevolence (2 Corinthians 4:18). Corrie ten Boom said, "When a train goes through a tunnel and it gets dark, you don't throw away the ticket and jump off. You sit still and trust the engineer."

> "The road is rugged, and the sun is hot. How can we be but weary? Here is grace for the weariness—grace which lifts us up and invigorates us...We receive of this grace, and are revived. Our weariness of heart and limb departs. We need no other refreshment. This is enough. Whatever the way be—rough, gloomy, unpleasant—we press forward, knowing that the same grace that has already carried thousands through will do the same for us."
>
> **Horatius Bonar**

DAY 51

Am I now trying to win the approval of human beings, or of God? Or am I trying to please people? If I were still trying to please people, I would not be a servant of Christ.

GALATIANS 1:10

We all seek approval—may we seek first the approval of *God* that's ours in Christ. He's the judge. We'll stand before his judgment seat, no one else's (2 Corinthians 5:10).

By all means, let's reach out with love and grace—but in the end, other people's opinions won't matter. Our opinions won't matter. God's opinion alone will matter, and his "opinion" is truth. He's the One we should seek to please, knowing that he is always pleased with Jesus, who is our righteousness at work in us (1 Corinthians 1:30).

> "The gospel brings me explosive news: my search for approval is over. In Christ I already have all the approval I need."
>
> **Dave Harvey**

DAY 52

*I consider that our present sufferings
are not worth comparing with the
glory that will be revealed in us.*

ROMANS 8:18

We should face the pains of this life infused with hope as we look forward to a glorious future with God in which the worst hardships here won't compare to the least joys there. Then we'll find grace and strength and encouragement to finish our course. "If God is for us, who can be against us?" (Romans 8:31).

J.A. Motyer wrote, "God is tirelessly on our side. He never falters in respect of our needs, he always has more grace at hand for us. He is never less than sufficient, he always has more and yet more to give."

> "If you can trust God to save you for eternity,
> you can trust him to lead you for a lifetime."
>
> **David Platt**

DAY 53

He said to me, "My grace is sufficient for you, for my power is made perfect in weakness." Therefore I will boast all the more gladly about my weaknesses, so that Christ's power may rest on me.

2 Corinthians 12:9

It's easy to be discouraged by our weaknesses. But Philip Hughes says, "The greater the servant's weakness, the more conspicuous is the power of his Master's all-sufficient grace."

We need Jesus just as much today as the day we first put our faith in him. Grace is more than a nice supplement that helps us now and then. Because we are weak, God's strengthening grace is a constant essential to the Christian life.

> "Every new duty calls for more grace than I now possess, but not more than is found in thee, the divine Treasury in whom all fullness dwells."

Puritan Prayer

DAY 54

They cried out to the Lord and said, "We have sinned; we have forsaken the Lord and served the Baals and the Ashtoreths. But now deliver us from the hands of our enemies, and we will serve you."

1 Samuel 12:10

How easily we dismiss God when things are going well, but how quickly we invoke his name and plead for his grace and mercy when we're desperate. Yet if we recognized God more in times of prosperity, we would be far better prepared for times of crisis.

> "When we grow careless of keeping our souls, God recovers our taste of good things by sharp crosses."
>
> **Richard Sibbes**

DAY 55

When the kindness and love of God our Savior appeared, he saved us, not because of righteous things we had done, but because of his mercy.

TITUS 3:4-5

Don't wonder why God might despise us—he has every reason to. Wonder why he loves us. Now that's incredible! It's not his wrath but his grace to us in Christ Jesus that's so surprising. Humans wonder how a loving God could send people to Hell. Righteous angels probably wonder how a just God made the way to bring people to Heaven.

"If we think we are not all that bad, the idea of grace will never change us. Change comes by seeing a need for a Savior and getting one."

Timothy Keller

DAY 56

*Let us not neglect our meeting together, as
some people do, but encourage one another.*

HEBREWS 10:25 (NLT)

A Christ-centered church isn't a display case for saints but
a hospital for sinners. All church people are flawed, but
most aren't self-righteous. Those who are should be pitied,
because they don't understand God's grace.

Ray Ortlund writes, "Gospel doctrine creates a gospel culture. The doctrine of grace creates a culture of
grace...Without the doctrine, the culture will be weak.
Without the culture, the doctrine will seem pointless."

Lord, grant your people not only the doctrine but the
culture of grace.

"The more I grow in grace the more
I see my need to grow in grace."

Burk Parsons

DAY 57

Rejoice always, pray continually, give thanks in all circumstances; for this is God's will for you in Christ Jesus.

1 THESSALONIANS 5:16-18

Christians in dire situations, undergoing persecution, are often deeply grateful for God's daily blessings. Yet some believers complain when traffic crawls or their omelet is overdone. We're quick to grumble about our circumstances, many of them insignificant.

In contrast, Scripture tells us, "Do all things without grumbling or disputing, that you may be blameless and innocent, children of God without blemish in the midst of a crooked and twisted generation, among whom you shine as lights in the world" (Philippians 2:14-15 ESV).

God, open our eyes to the wonders of your grace, which eclipses all the reasons for our complaints.

"You will never develop character by running from unpleasant situations."

Dallas Willard

DAY 58

Go and learn what this means:
"I desire mercy, not sacrifice."
For I have not come to call
the righteous, but sinners.

MATTHEW 9:13

I invited a lesbian activist to lunch. While we ate, she raised her voice and cursed freely as she told me about Christians who'd mistreated her. People stared. But that was OK. Jesus went to the cross for her—the least I could do was listen.

Then suddenly she was sobbing, broken. The next two hours I heard her story, her heartsickness, her doubts about the causes she championed. I told her about Christ's grace.

We walked out of that restaurant as friends, four hours later, side by side, smiling.

> "The way to open our hearts to others is
> by receiving afresh the grace of God and
> appreciating what it means: seeing our own
> need of Christ; coming to receive his mercy;
> sensing how undeserved his love for us is."
>
> Sinclair Ferguson

DAY 59

But the tax collector stood at a distance. He would not even look up to heaven, but beat his breast and said, "God, have mercy on me, a sinner." I tell you that this man, rather than the other, went home justified before God.

LUKE 18:13-14

Those who know their unworthiness reach for grace as the thirsty reach for water. Meanwhile, the self-righteous resent grace. Why do they need God's grace when they believe they're "good enough" on their own?

> "Brokenness is the stripping of self-reliance and independence from God. The broken person has no confidence in his own righteousness or his own works, but he is cast in total dependence upon the grace of God working in and through him."
>
> Nancy Leigh DeMoss

DAY 60

Those who listen to instruction will prosper;
those who trust the LORD will be joyful.

PROVERBS 16:20 (NLT)

God remains sovereign and loving and purposeful even when he has designs other than the ones I wished for—"according to the plan of him who works out everything in conformity with the purpose of his will" (Ephesians 1:11).

Corrie ten Boom, who lived in a prison camp for years, said, "Every experience God gives us, every person he puts in our lives is the perfect preparation for the future that only he can see."

One day we'll see in retrospect that all along he was working all things together for our good (Romans 8:28). May God give us the grace to believe today what we will one day know and see to have been true all along.

"Everything is necessary that God sends our way;
nothing can be necessary that he withholds."

John Newton

DAY 61

Great are the works of the LORD;
they are pondered by all who delight in them.

PSALM 111:2

Getting in touch every day with God's grace, learning to thank him for the small things, serves us well when we lose big things. It deepens our reservoir and gives us eyes to see God's faithfulness and blessings at a time when we most need clear vision.

John MacArthur writes, "Grace upholds our salvation, gives us victory in temptation, and helps us endure suffering and pain. It helps us understand the Word and wisely apply it to our lives. It draws us into communion and prayer and enables us to serve the Lord effectively. In short, we exist and are firmly fixed in an environment of all-sufficient grace."

> "It's impossible to exaggerate the
> gospel. Hyperbole never applies
> to the riches of God's grace."
>
> **Scotty Smith**

Indeed, we felt we had received the sentence of death. But this happened that we might not rely on ourselves but on God, who raises the dead.

2 Corinthians 1:9

Suffering can serve as the hard, cold wakeup call that tells us how helpless we are without God. Though it does not appear to be a grace, suffering can lead us to repentance and humility and trust in God. Samuel Rutherford said, "Grace grows best in winter."

Grace invisible or disguised is nonetheless grace.

"God will not protect you from anything
that will make you more like Jesus."

Elisabeth Elliot

DAY 63

Lovingkindness and truth have met together;
righteousness and peace have kissed each other.

PSALM 85:10 (NASB)

Christ's heart is equally grieved by grace-suppression and truth-suppression, by grace-twisting and truth-twisting. Truth without grace is legalism. Grace without truth is deception. Without truth there is no need for salvation. Without grace there is no hope for salvation.

Since Jesus was the perfect embodiment of grace and truth, we can't bring glory to Christ by separating the two. We must embrace a gospel that is as full of grace and truth as Jesus is.

> "Truth without grace is bullying and aggressive. Grace without truth is codependent and enabling."
>
> **Scott Sauls**

DAY 64

You are the God who performs miracles;
you display your power among the peoples.

PSALM 77:14

I frequently learn new things about my wife, daughters, grandkids, and closest friends, though I've known them for years. If I can always be learning something new about finite, limited human beings, surely I'll learn far more about Jesus on the New Earth. None of us will ever exhaust his depths of grace.

> "To be loved but not known is comforting but superficial. To be known and not loved is our greatest fear. But to be fully known and truly loved is, well, a lot like being loved by God."

Timothy Keller

DAY 65

If you, LORD, kept a record of sins,
Lord, who could stand?
But with you there is forgiveness,
so that we can, with reverence, serve you.
I wait for the LORD, my whole being waits,
and in his word I put my hope.

PSALM 130:3-5

When you love someone, you don't want them to sin because it's never in their best interests. Sin brings judgment and misery, and we don't want loved ones to fall under God's judgment. Rather, we want them to embrace the forgiving grace Christ offers through the cross. Grace doesn't minimize or ignore sin. Rather, it faces sin head-on, pays for it, forgives it, and conquers it.

> "As heat is opposed to cold, and light to darkness, so grace is opposed to sin. Fire and water may as well agree in the same vessel, as grace and sin in the same heart."
>
> Thomas Brooks

DAY 66

It is written: "Be holy, because I am holy."

1 PETER 1:16

J.I. Packer writes, "Holiness is always the saved sinner's response of gratitude for grace received." But many professing Christians celebrate a pseudo-liberty characterized by an ever-increasing tolerance for sin. This is not grace.

Bryan Chapell says, "Resting on God's grace does not relieve us of our holy obligations; rather it should enable us to fulfill them."

It's entirely possible, by our Lord's gracious empowerment, to live in a way that will one day prompt him to say, "Well done, my good and faithful servant."

> "Cheap grace is the deadly enemy of our church. Cheap grace means grace sold on the market...Cheap grace is the preaching of forgiveness without requiring repentance...Cheap grace is grace without discipleship, grace without the cross, grace without Jesus Christ, living and incarnate."
>
> **Dietrich Bonhoeffer**

DAY 67

Look! God's dwelling place is now among the people, and he will dwell with them. They will be his people, and God himself will be with them and be their God. He will wipe every tear from their eyes. There will be no more death or mourning or crying or pain.

REVELATION 21:3-4

"Everyone lived happily ever after" is not just a fairytale ending. It's God's promise to his children. As C.S. Lewis wrote in *The Last Battle*, ours is a story "which no one on earth has read: which goes on forever: in which every chapter is better than the one before."

"Heaven is real because God, in utter grace,
has made a way for his sinful creatures
to return to him, and to live with him in
everlasting righteousness and joy."

George Raymond Beasley-Murray

DAY 68

Strengthen me according to your word.

PSALM 119:28

God's Word is a daily source of joy to me. Any day I fail to mull over Scripture, contemplating and worshipping my Lord, my happiness is invariably diminished. I tend to be more impatient and critical. Something is wrong—and that something is my lack of God's fresh infusion of grace through his Word.

C.S. Lewis wrote, "If you want to get warm you must stand near the fire. If you want joy, peace, eternal life, you must get close to what has them."

> "It is the word of God alone which can first and effectually cheer the heart of any sinner. There is no true or solid peace to be enjoyed in the world except in the way of reposing upon the promises of God."
>
> **John Calvin**

DAY 69

One thing I ask from the LORD,
this only do I seek:
that I may dwell in the house of the LORD
all the days of my life,
to gaze on the beauty of the LORD
and to seek him in his temple.

PSALM 27:4

Let's learn to look at the complete Jesus revealed in Scripture, not refashion him with love—that is, our definition of love—as his only attribute. By seeing him in his holiness *and* love, truth *and* grace, we behold his full majesty. God is always more beautiful than our attempts to airbrush and reshape him to fit the spirit of the age.

> "God could have set up a throne of strict justice, dispensing death to all who were convened before it...God has, instead, chosen to set up a throne of grace...There, at that throne, grace reigns, and acts with sovereign freedom, power, and bounty."
>
> Joni Eareckson Tada

DAY 70

*They tell how you turned to God from idols to serve
the living and true God, and to wait for his Son
from heaven, whom he raised from the dead—
Jesus, who rescues us from the coming wrath.*

1 THESSALONIANS 1:9-10

Some Christians are now waffling on the reality of Hell,
reinterpreting Scripture, trying to be culturally popular
and cover for God to improve his ratings. They do this in
the name of grace. But true love tells the truth. Instead of
asking why God sends people to Hell, we ought to be asking why he would save any of us. The answer is grace. And
grace loses its value if there is nothing from which to be
saved.

> "The cross is the lightning rod of grace that
> short-circuits God's wrath to Christ so that only
> the light of his love remains for believers."
>
> A.W. Tozer

DAY 71

*I was given a thorn in my flesh, a messenger of
Satan, to torment me. Three times I pleaded
with the Lord to take it away from me. But he
said to me, "My grace is sufficient for you, for my
power is made perfect in weakness." Therefore
I will boast all the more gladly about my
weaknesses, so that Christ's power may rest on me.*

2 CORINTHIANS 12:7-9

How often have we prayed that God would make us Christlike, then begged him to take away the very things he sent to make us Christlike? How many times has he said no to our prayers because saying yes would harm us and rob us of good? His grace is sufficient as we face life's greatest difficulties. He knows better than we do—always.

> "God knows every detail of your past
> sins and present situation. And his
> grace is sufficient for both."
>
> David Jeremiah

DAY 72

It is the LORD your God you must follow, and him you must revere. Keep his commands and obey him; serve him and hold fast to him.

DEUTERONOMY 13:4

The message that God in his grace can forgive and "bestow on [his people] a crown of beauty instead of ashes" (Isaiah 61:3) is wonderfully true. But that's a message for those who *have* sinned, not those contemplating sin. We must call upon both the love of God and the fear of God, which act in concert, motivating us to holy obedience.

Bryan Chapell says, "If our teaching of grace causes us to make light of sin, or to slight the requirements of the Savior, then we have not really understood either the monstrosity of our sin or the greatness of the heart that forgives it."

"The heart that has really tasted the grace of Christ will instinctively hate sin."

J.C. Ryle

DAY 73

The centurion replied, "Lord, I do not deserve
to have you come under my roof. But just say
the word, and my servant will be healed."

MATTHEW 8:8

William Farley modifies a well-known acronym: "GRACE
is God's Riches At Christ's Expense *extended to men and*
women who deserve wrath." That makes it a fully biblical
statement.

The Roman centurion sent word to Jesus: "I did not
even consider myself worthy to come to you" (Luke 7:6-7).
We are never thankful for what we think we deserve. We
are always deeply thankful for great kindness we know we
don't deserve.

> "The measure of God's love for us is shown
> by two things. One is the degree of his
> sacrifice in saving us from the penalty of our
> sin. The other is the degree of unworthiness
> that we had when he saved us."
>
> John Piper

DAY 74

Pride goes before destruction,
a haughty spirit before a fall.

PROVERBS 16:18

When we imagine we're special, that we've earned people's respect, that we have a lot to offer, then we become proud. That means God is opposed to us, since he "opposes the proud, but gives grace to the humble" (James 4:6 NLT). Whenever we admire and exalt ourselves, we're operating outside of his grace. That makes us, every time, a fall waiting to happen.

> "We cannot find God without God. We cannot reach God without God. We cannot satisfy God without God...The secret of the quest lies not in our brilliance but in his grace."
>
> **Os Guinness**

DAY 75

Therefore, there is now no condemnation for those who are in Christ Jesus, because through Christ Jesus the law of the Spirit who gives life has set you free from the law of sin and death.

ROMANS 8:1-2

It's only part of the story to say God loves us just the way we are. God also loves us too much to leave us that way. We're not basically good people. We're sinners in desperate need of grace. But the gospel, the Good News, is that God offers that very grace without which we have no hope. He cleanses us from our guilt and gives us the only valid basis for a positive self-image. Once God has declared us "not guilty," he says there is no condemnation for us!

> "A changing life is a cross-centered life...At the cross we find the grace, power, and delight in God we need to overcome sin."
>
> Tim Chester

DAY 76

*The Word became flesh and made
his dwelling among us.*

JOHN 1:14

A.W. Tozer wrote, "The grace of God is infinite and eternal. As it had no beginning, so it can have no end."

Jesus said to his disciples, "Learn from me" (Matthew 11:29). In Heaven we'll go ever deeper in our understanding of God's grace and kindness (Ephesians 2:7).

Jesus is a living book—"the Word"—which we'll continue to "read" forever. We'll never get to the end of him, but will forever eagerly turn the next page.

> "We often feel as if grace had done its utmost
> when it has carried us safely through the desert
> and set us down at the gate of the kingdom...But
> the love that shall meet us then to bid us
> welcome to the many mansions, shall be love
> beyond what we were here able to comprehend."
>
> **Horatius Bonar**

DAY 77

*Live as children of light (for the fruit of the
light consists in all goodness, righteousness and
truth) and find out what pleases the Lord.*

Ephesians 5:8-10

Thomas Goodwin wrote, "Now God, who is an infinite Sovereign, who might have chosen whether ever he would love us or no, for him to love us, this is grace."

Yes! May we grow deeper in our love for Jesus, honoring him in our choices, quick to call upon his grace, remembering always the permanent marks of his love, for us, forever displayed on his hands and feet.

"The grace of Christ is not an excuse for
weakness; he is an endless resource for strength."

Ray Ortlund

DAY 78

See to it that no one falls short of the grace of God and that no bitter root grows up to cause trouble and defile many.

HEBREWS 12:15

Bitterness and resentment are the heavy price we pay for minimizing our sins against God and dwelling on others' sins against us (to do the one is to do the other). Ultimately, the one thing costlier than forgiving is not forgiving. Nothing does us and the body of Christ more harm.

Scott Hafemann says, "The heart that is opened to receive the grace of Christ will learn to welcome all those whom Christ himself has welcomed."

> "The ability to forgive is one of the surest signs of having been forgiven. It is part of the proof that we have received God's grace...Those who are truly forgiven, truly forgive. The sins they commit are of greater importance to them than the sins they suffer."
>
> Philip Ryken

DAY 79

Abraham replied, "Son, remember that in your lifetime you received your good things, while Lazarus received bad things, but now he is comforted here and you are in agony."

LUKE 16:25

Memory is a basic element of personality. To be truly ourselves in Heaven, there must be continuity of memory from Earth to Heaven. We will not be different people, but the same people marvelously relocated and transformed. Undoubtedly we'll remember God's works of grace in our lives that comforted, assured, sustained, and empowered us to live for him.

> "How much there will be to talk about! What wondrous wisdom will appear in everything that we had to go through in the days of our flesh! We shall remember all the way by which we were led, and say, 'Goodness and mercy followed me all the days of my life.'"
>
> J.C. Ryle

DAY 80

*Sin shall no longer be your master, because
you are not under the law, but under grace.*

ROMANS 6:14

Grace doesn't make people less holy; it makes them more
holy. Grace doesn't make people despise truth; it makes
them love and follow truth. Far from a free pass to sin,
grace is a cleansing that brings a supernatural empowerment not to sin. Richard Sibbes said, "There is more mercy
in Christ than sin in us."

Nearly everyone longs to see more grace in the church.
May it start today not just with others, but with us. Philip
Yancey writes, "I rejected the church for a time because I
found so little grace there. I returned because I found grace
nowhere else."

> "Will you live today like grace has connected
> your life to something vastly bigger than the
> hopes and dreams of this little moment?"
>
> Paul Tripp

DAY 81

*Your name and renown
are the desire of our hearts.*

Isaiah 26:8

Augustine wrote, "You have made us for yourself, O Lord, and our heart is restless until it rests in you." Ultimate satisfaction can be found in God alone, the Creator and gracious giver of all goodness. We were made for him and we'll never be satisfied with less than him. Coming to grips with this happy thought is one of the great keys to Christian living.

> "Give a man everything that this world can give...something *is wanting*! That *something* is neither more nor less than the knowledge and love of God; without which no spirit can be happy either in heaven or earth."
>
> **John Wesley**

DAY 82

*What do you have that you did not
receive? And if you did receive it, why
do you boast as though you did not?*

1 CORINTHIANS 4:7

How gracious of God to put us in positions of need so that
we may experience the joy of receiving from his hand. Not
only the gifts he's given us to serve him and others, but each
and every breath is a grace from God. And if every heart-
beat is a gift from his hand, how much more the flood of
redemptive grace in Jesus?

> "Ungodly men prosper well enough in this
> world. They root themselves, and spread
> themselves like green bay trees: this world is
> their native soil; but the Christian needs the
> greenhouse of grace to keep himself alive at all."
>
> Charles Spurgeon

DAY 83

Jesus answered, "I am the way and the truth and the life. No one comes to the Father except through me."

JOHN 14:6

God is gracious and loving enough to tell us the truth. There are two eternal destinations, not one. We must choose the right path if we're to go to Heaven. All roads do not lead to Heaven, only one: Jesus Christ. We cannot build the road; he already did. We are blind and cannot find the road without his guiding hand. Once on it, we can only walk it by his strength.

> "The gospel is not a way to get people to heaven; it is a way to get people to God...If we don't want God above all things, we have not been converted by the gospel."
>
> John Piper

DAY 84

*From his fullness we have all
received, grace upon grace.*

JOHN 1:16 (ESV)

Most sinners loved being around Jesus. They enjoyed his company and sought him out. Today most sinners don't want to be around Christians. Unbelievers tore off the roof to get to Jesus. Why? What did Jesus show them that we don't? *Grace.* People sensed that Jesus loved them, even when he spoke difficult words that reminded them of their sin.

> "No one else holds or has held the place in the heart of the world which Jesus holds. Other gods have been as devoutly worshipped; no other man has been so devoutly loved."
>
> **John Knox**

DAY 85

*Then, after desire has conceived, it
gives birth to sin; and sin, when it is
full-grown, gives birth to death.*

JAMES 1:15

Erwin Lutzer says, "There is more grace in God's heart than
there is sin in your past." As we grow closer to Christ, and
increase in our knowledge of him and his grace, we see sin
for what it is. Gradually, it loses its hold on us—largely
because we see the misery it brings. Sin? Been there, done
that. Who in his right mind would want more of it?

> "The victorious Christian neither exalts
> nor downgrades himself. His interests
> have shifted from self to Christ."
>
> **A.W. Tozer**

DAY 86

Therefore, as God's chosen people, holy and dearly loved, clothe yourselves with compassion, kindness, humility, gentleness and patience.

COLOSSIANS 3:12

If we are broken, humble, quick to admit and confess our weaknesses and sins, God will shed his grace upon us, comfort us, and empower us. Then, and only then, we will be Christlike and Christ-exalting.

John Piper says, "There is no other object of knowledge in the universe that exposes proud, man-exalting thinking like the cross does. Only humble, Christ-exalting thinking can survive in the presence of the cross. The effect of the cross on our thinking is not to cut off thinking about God, but to confound boasting in the presence of God. The cross does not nullify thinking, it purifies thinking."

"The sufficiency of my merit is to know that my merit is not sufficient."

Saint Augustine

DAY 87

"Then neither do I condemn you," Jesus
declared. "Go now and leave your life of sin."

JOHN 8:11

"Hate the sin, but love the sinner." The expression may seem trite because it is used so often. (And we should hate our *own* sin the most!) Yet this expression has merit, and no one fulfilled it better than Jesus, about whom Jonathan Edwards asked, "What is there that you could desire in a Savior that is not in Christ?" Truth hates sin. Grace loves sinners. Those full of grace and truth—those full of Jesus— do both.

"You're the only gospel many people will ever read. So show grace and truth."

Charles Swindoll

DAY 88

*This grace was given us in Christ Jesus
before the beginning of time.*

2 TIMOTHY 1:9

God wrote the script of this drama of grace-filled redemption an eternity before Satan, demons, Adam and Eve—and you and I—took the stage. And from the beginning, he knew that the utterly spectacular ending (without end) would make the dark middle worth it.

God has his hands on Earth. He will not let go. The nails that pierced his hands secured him to Earth and its eternal future. In a redemptive work far greater than we imagine, Christ bought and paid for both our future and Earth's.

"Praise be to his glorious name forever; may the whole earth be filled with his glory. Amen and Amen" (Psalm 72:19).

> "Welcome, welcome, cross of
> Christ, if Christ be with it."
>
> **Samuel Rutherford**

DAY 89

So then, just as you received Christ Jesus as Lord,
continue to live your lives in him, rooted and
built up in him, strengthened in the faith as you
were taught, and overflowing with thankfulness.

Colossians 2:6-7

Perhaps the greatest heritage parents can pass on to their children is the ability to perceive the multitude of our gracious God's daily blessings and to respond with continual gratitude.

We should be "overflowing with thankfulness." When we are, we'll also be overflowing with the joy of Jesus, making the gospel as attractive as "the good news of happiness" should be (Isaiah 52:7 ESV). Because God's grace is constant, new, and fresh, our gratitude should be constant, new, and fresh.

> "The Lord Jesus is a deep sea of joy: my
> soul shall dive therein, shall be swallowed
> up in the delights of his society."
>
> Charles Spurgeon

DAY 90

Do not be anxious about anything, but
in every situation, by prayer and petition,
with thanksgiving, present your requests
to God. And the peace of God, which
transcends all understanding, will guard
your hearts and your minds in Christ Jesus.

PHILIPPIANS 4:6-7

If you pray in light of God's sovereign grace and unfailing love, your anxiety will eventually give way to peace. He listens to us and knows how to give us good gifts, including his Holy Spirit (Luke 11:13).

We're told, "He who did not spare his own Son, but gave him up for us all—how will he not also, along with him, graciously give us all things?" (Romans 8:32).

All things begin and end with grace. It never lets you want to go back to the barren wasteland of ingratitude. "Enter his gates with thanksgiving" (Psalm 100:4).

"Prayer is always a suitable response to grace."

Ed Welch

DAY 91

*Since the children have flesh and blood, he
too shared in their humanity so that by
his death he might break the power of him
who holds the power of death—that is, the
devil—and free those who all their lives
were held in slavery by their fear of death.*

HEBREWS 2:14-15

If we build our lives on the solid foundation of Jesus's redemptive work, we should all be optimists. Even our most painful experiences in life are temporary setbacks, every obstacle an opportunity for his sovereign grace to deliver us.

Augustine prayed, "Give me the grace to do as You command, and command me to do what You will...when Your commands are obeyed, it is from You that we receive the power to obey them."

"The empty tomb of Jesus tells you that
there is nothing that has the power to
defeat God's plan of redeeming grace."

Paul Tripp

DAY 92

In their hearts humans plan their course,
but the LORD establishes their steps.

PROVERBS 16:9

Hundreds of millions of choices and actions are contemplated every second across this globe. Our God, who is all-knowing, all-powerful, and full of grace, chooses exactly which ones he'll cause or not, ordain or not, permit or not. Everything he permits coincides with his wisdom and ultimately serves his holiness, justice, and love.

To top it off, this great, sovereign, and all-wise God is our Father, who acts in the best interests of his children (Romans 8:15).

> "If you want to judge how well a person understands Christianity, find out how much he makes of the thought of being God's child, and having God as his Father."
>
> J.I. Packer

DAY 93

He will swallow up death forever.
The Sovereign LORD will wipe away the tears
from all faces;
he will remove his people's disgrace
from all the earth.
The LORD has spoken.

ISAIAH 25:8

Through the redemptive suffering of Christ—taking all human evils on himself—and through his triumph over evil and death, God in his grace has done everything necessary to defeat evil. One day he'll carry out his final redemptive work, comforting forever the hearts of all his children.

"The devil will shrink back in defeat. The angels will step forward in awe. And we saints will stand tall in God's grace. As we see how much he has forgiven us, we will see how much he loves us. And we will worship him."

Max Lucado

DAY 94

Yet because the wicked do not fear
God, it will not go well with them.

ECCLESIASTES 8:13

God is gracious, good, and loving. But we need to acknowledge that he is not predictable, nor is he in any sense under our control. We can't say the magic words or call upon him like he's our genie. Until we come to grips with the truth of his uncompromising majesty, independence, and holiness, we'll never begin to grasp his amazing grace.

> "'Safe?' said Mr. Beaver; 'don't you hear
> what Mrs. Beaver tells you? Who said
> anything about safe? Course he isn't safe.
> But he's good. He's the King, I tell you.'"
>
> C.S. Lewis

DAY 95

You make known to me the path of life;
you will fill me with joy in your presence,
with eternal pleasures at your right hand.

PSALM 16:11

Joy and delight surround God. People who reject him now can maintain the illusion that life is good without him only because, in his kindness, he hasn't withdrawn all his gifts. But all people desperately need his redeeming grace.

Spurgeon said, "Nowhere does the soul ever find such consolation as on that very spot where misery reigned, where woe triumphed, where agony reached its climax. There grace has dug a fountain, which ever gushes with waters pure as crystal, each drop capable of alleviating the woes and the agonies of mankind."

"Let wrath deserved
be written on the door of hell,
But the free gift of grace on the gate of heaven."

Puritan Prayer

DAY 96

Read Luke 1 and 2, and marvel at the redemptive work of our Father, sending his Son, our Savior, into this world. He did it for us. Weep at the sheer power of God's amazing grace and the greatness of his eternity-shaping plan. When next you celebrate Christmas—which God's people can celebrate daily—may you enjoy his sovereign grace and clearly sense his steadfast love for you.

"There's nothing like creating the real Christmas spirit by focusing on just why you need a Savior—why you desperately need Jesus. Oh, thank you Jesus for coming and bringing your light into our dark world."

Joni Eareckson Tada

DAY 97

I am the vine; you are the branches. If you remain in me and I in you, you will bear much fruit; apart from me you can do nothing.

JOHN 15:5

Followers of Christ too often live as if we can get by without God's all-powerful grace. If we don't have a clear picture of what's ahead of us in eternity, then we'll think, *I'll just grab onto this life now and do whatever I think will make me happy.*

Nothing could be more shortsighted in light of the long tomorrow.

> "Rivet your soul on the grace that you will receive when Christ returns. Tolerate no distractions. Entertain no diversions...Devote every ounce of mental and spiritual and emotional energy to concentrating and contemplating on the grace that is to come. What grace is that? It is the grace of the heavenly inheritance."
>
> **Sam Storms**

DAY 98

Ascribe to the LORD the glory due his name;
bring an offering and come before him.
Worship the LORD in the splendor of his holiness.

1 CHRONICLES 16:29

God's people are called upon to honor and worship the One whose name is above all names. That means we must identify and reject the false gods celebrated by our culture. "Those who cling to worthless idols turn away from God's love for them" (Jonah 2:8).

May we exalt the true Jesus, full of grace and truth, as he's revealed in Scripture, and turn away from the pseudo-christs remade in our image.

"Dear children, keep yourselves from idols" (1 John 5:21).

> "Sin causes our hearts to replace God with something else; grace works to restore God to his rightful place."
>
> Paul Tripp

DAY 99

That is why, for Christ's sake, I delight in
weaknesses, in insults, in hardships, in
persecutions, in difficulties. For when
I am weak, then I am strong.

2 CORINTHIANS 12:10

God uses our weaknesses and inadequacy not only to build our characters, but to manifest his strength and grace. So I see his goodness in giving me certain weaknesses (including insulin-dependent diabetes) to accomplish his good purposes. I'll not wait to celebrate those purposes in eternity; I'm celebrating them now.

"My God, I have never thanked you for my thorn!
I have thanked you a thousand times for my
roses, but never once for my thorn...Teach
me the value of my thorns...Show me
that my tears have made my rainbow."

George Matheson

DAY 100

*The God of all grace, who called you to his
eternal glory in Christ, after you have suffered
a little while, will himself restore you and
make you strong, firm and steadfast.*

1 PETER 5:10

As believers in Christ, our theology gives us perspective.
We learn this life is the preface—not the book. The pre-
liminaries—not the main event. The tune-up—not the
concert.

I've talked with many people who've been diagnosed
with terminal diseases. They have a sudden and insatiable
interest in Heaven. Most people live unprepared for death.
But the wise will discover how their choices during their brief
stay here matter in eternity, and adjust them accordingly.

> "The settled happiness and security which
> we all desire, God withholds from us
> by the very nature of the world: but joy,
> pleasure, and merriment, He has scattered
> broadcast...Our Father refreshes us on the
> journey with some pleasant inns, but will not
> encourage us to mistake them for home."
>
> C.S. Lewis

DAY 101

Blessed are you who weep now,
for you will laugh.

LUKE 6:21

Puritan John Owen wrote, "A man may take the measure of his growth and decay in grace according to his thoughts and meditations upon the person of Christ."

When you face difficulty and discouragement, keep your eyes on joy's Source. Recite Christ's gracious promise for the new world, a promise that echoes off the far reaches of the universe.

"Joy is to be found in Heaven now by anticipation and later by realization. Joyful are those people who have two feet upon the earth, but who breathe Heaven's air."

Steven J. Lawson

DAY 102

*[Christ] entered heaven itself, now to appear
for us in God's presence...He will appear a
second time, not to bear sin, but to bring
salvation to those who are waiting for him.*

HEBREWS 9:24,28

The God who lives in unapproachable light became
approachable in the person of Jesus. Though we'll always
be the creatures and he the Creator, in Heaven we'll live
with him and actually see his face. All as a result of his
mind-boggling grace!

> "Christ did not die to forgive sinners who go on
> treasuring anything above seeing and savoring
> God. And people who would be happy in
> heaven if Christ were not there, will not be there."
>
> John Piper

DAY 103

We, however, will not boast beyond proper limits, but will confine our boasting to the sphere of service God himself has assigned to us, a sphere that also includes you.

2 Corinthians 10:13

God in his grace has given each of us our own unique sphere of influence to use for our Lord. So how are we using it?

Jerry Bridges writes, "We could not take one step in the pursuit of holiness if God in his grace had not first delivered us from the dominion of sin and brought us into union with his risen Son. Salvation is by grace and sanctification is by grace."

The grace that saves and sanctifies is the same grace that enables us to serve him in our unique place—to make an eternal difference *by* him and *for* him.

> "I value all things only by the price they shall gain in eternity."
>
> John Wesley

DAY 104

My God will meet all your needs according to the riches of his glory in Christ Jesus.

PHILIPPIANS 4:19

As we learn to give, we draw closer to the God whose grace is the fount of all giving. But no matter how much we grow in the grace of giving, Jesus Christ remains the matchless giver: "For you know the grace of our Lord Jesus Christ, that though he was rich, yet for your sake he became poor, so that you through his poverty might become rich" (2 Corinthians 8:9). May God extend his grace not only to us, but through us to those around us who need God's grace above all else.

> "Grace and gratitude belong together like heaven and earth. Grace evokes gratitude like the voice an echo. Gratitude follows grace as thunder follows lightning."
>
> **Karl Barth**

DAY 105

*To the LORD your God belong the heavens, even
the highest heavens, the earth and everything in it.*

DEUTERONOMY 10:14

When our girls were young, Nanci and I knew we shouldn't
sacrifice them for God's kingdom, but we learned it's good
to make sacrifices for his kingdom *with* our children. We
were able to walk that path only because of a lesson he'd
already taught us: everything—including our children—
belongs to him. As his grace is sufficient for us, it is sufficient for our children and all whom we love.

Dietrich Bonhoeffer wrote, "Grace is *costly* because it
calls us to follow, and it is *grace* because it calls us to follow
Jesus Christ. It is costly because it costs a man his life, and it
is grace because it gives a man the only true life."

"You don't realize God is all you
need until God is all you have."

Timothy Keller

DAY 106

*He causes his sun to rise on the evil
and the good, and sends rain on the
righteous and the unrighteous.*

MATTHEW 5:45

Even in this world under the curse, by God's grace, human imagination and skill have produced some remarkable works. Beethoven's Ninth Symphony. The Golden Gate Bridge. Baseball. Heart transplants. Prenatal surgery. The space shuttle. Chocolate ice cream. It's a list that never ends.

With the resources God will lavishly give us on the New Earth, what will we be able to accomplish together for his eternal glory?

> "What we need is not to be rescued from the world, not to cease being human, not to stop caring for the world, not to stop shaping human culture. What we need is the power to do these things according to the will of God. We, as well as the rest of creation, need to be redeemed."

> Paul Marshall

DAY 107

*I am the LORD your God, who brought you
out of Egypt, out of the land of slavery.*

EXODUS 20:2

God regularly reminds his people of his past acts of faithfulness. History, when viewed accurately, teaches us about God and about ourselves. It's the record of our failure to rule the earth righteously, the record of God's sovereign and gracious redemption of us and our planet.

We should remember and reflect on God's works in order to have faith that he's at work today and will be tomorrow, regardless of the difficulties we face.

"God is true. His Word of Promise is sure.
In all his relations with his people God is
faithful. He may be safely relied upon. No
one ever yet really trusted him in vain."

A.W. Pink

DAY 108

[Trials] have come so that the proven genuineness of your faith—of greater worth than gold, which perishes even though refined by fire—may result in praise, glory and honor when Jesus Christ is revealed.

1 Peter 1:7

Just like the individual ingredients that become a chocolate cake, the individual ingredients of trials and apparent tragedies can taste bitter to us. But our God of sovereign grace carefully measures out and mixes all the components of our lives, introduces just the right amount of heat, and produces a wonderful final product: our ultimate good for his ultimate glory.

> "Trials are medicines which our gracious and wise physician prescribes because we need them; and he proportions the frequency and weight of them to what the case requires. Let us trust in his skill and thank him for his prescription."
>
> John Newton

DAY 109

*Far be it from you to do such a thing—to kill
the righteous with the wicked, treating the
righteous and the wicked alike. Far be it from
you! Will not the Judge of all the earth do right?*

GENESIS 18:25

God is both just and gracious. "Will not the Judge of all
the earth do right?" Abram asked. It's a rhetorical question that assumes and demands a yes answer. Because we
know he'll always do right, we needn't worry that some
ultimate wrong will slip through his fingers without facing his judgment.

Each part of our lives is being used for his glory through
amazing works of his sovereign grace. Our faith should
never be in our faith, but only in our magnificent, promise-
keeping God.

> "It is not the strength of your faith but the
> object of your faith that actually saves you."
>
> Timothy Keller

DAY 110

"For I know the plans I have for you," declares
the LORD, "plans to prosper you and not
to harm you, plans to give you hope and
a future... You will seek me and find me
when you seek me with all your heart."

JEREMIAH 29:11,13

The Father directs his universe according to an eternal plan in which he lavished upon us in Christ a purifying love—for his everlasting glory and our everlasting good.

He makes no guarantees of short-term health and prosperity, but God has secured with his blood our eternal welfare and never-ending happiness. By his grace we can frontload that future happiness into our lives right now.

> "Were it not for God's restraining hand, we'd
> see *much* more violence, natural catastrophes,
> war and crime...And because of God's grace,
> because of his hope and promises, aren't you
> glad to know that one day, things *will* get better?"
>
> Joni Eareckson Tada

DAY 111

*Heaven must receive [Jesus] until the time
comes for God to restore everything, as he
promised long ago through his holy prophets.*

Acts 3:21

Sometimes, there really are no words to say to others and
ourselves in the midst of great grief. But there remains
the Word, Jesus the Son of God, the expression of God's
fullness (Colossians 2:9). He is Immanuel, God with us.
He didn't just send an angel. No one but Jesus was good
enough.

This same Jesus told his disciples "at the renewal of all
things, when the Son of Man sits on his glorious throne,
you who have followed me will also sit on twelve thrones"
(Matthew 19:28). How far does his redemptive grace
extend? He promised to renew the universe itself!

> "The grace that restores is necessary to
> preserve, lead, guard, supply, help me."
>
> Puritan Prayer

DAY 112

Can a mother forget the baby at her breast
and have no compassion
on the child she has borne?
Though she may forget, I will not forget you!
See, I have engraved you on the palms of my hands.

Isaiah 49:15-16

God cannot forget us or fail to have compassion on us, his children, even if the best of mothers ever could. God will never under any circumstances fail us. By his sovereign love and grace, God has permanently fixed us on his hands. "God has said, 'Never will I leave you; never will I forsake you'" (Hebrews 13:5).

> "There is nothing more acceptable to the Father than for us to keep up our hearts unto him as the eternal fountain of all that rich grace which flows out to sinners in the blood of Jesus."
>
> **John Owen**

DAY 113

Shall we go on sinning so that grace may increase? By no means! We are those who have died to sin; how can we live in it any longer?

ROMANS 6:1-2

We might explain away sin by saying "That's not what I meant" or "I did what my father always did to me" or "I wouldn't have done this if you hadn't done that." These statements minimize our evil and thereby minimize God's greatness in atoning for it.

"If he were shorthanded with his love, what would become of us? If he had but little graciousness, if he had but little glory, then we great sinners must certainly perish. But since the Lord is a bottomless well of love and a topless mountain of grace, we may come to him, and come freely, without any fear that either his grace or his glory will ever suffer any diminution."

Charles Spurgeon

DAY 114

May all who seek you
rejoice and be glad in you;
may those who love your salvation
say continually, "Great is the LORD!"

PSALM 40:16 (ESV)

We come to Christ empty-handed. We can take no credit for salvation. Yet once we're saved, though he doesn't need our gifts, he welcomes them as parents welcome gifts from their children.

What gift are you giving Jesus? Our love, worship, awe, time spent with him, being yielded to him, and being committed to follow him wherever he leads—these are gifts he treasures. They are our lesser but nonetheless precious responses to God's greater grace to us. Our heartfelt gift of praise and thanks pleases God and makes us happy too.

> "Faith means not doing something but
> receiving something; it means not the earning
> of a reward but the acceptance of a gift."
>
> J. Gresham Machen

DAY 115

Join with me in suffering for the gospel, by the
power of God. He has saved us and called us to
a holy life—not because of anything we have
done but because of his own purpose and grace.

2 TIMOTHY 1:8-9

God's holiness is sufficient reason for us to be holy, but
his holiness alone doesn't make us live holy lives. His saving and sanctifying grace is our means to holiness. God is
our empowerment for holiness. Many of us rightly believe
we should be more holy, but attempting to be holy in our
strength, and for our glory, is to be unholy. To be holy in
Christ's strength and for his glory...that's our calling and
our joy.

> "God sees us perfect in his Son while he
> disciplines and chastens and purges us
> that we may be partakers of his holiness."

A.W. Tozer

DAY 116

But I, with shouts of grateful praise,
will sacrifice to you.
What I have vowed I will make good.
I will say, "Salvation comes from the LORD."

JONAH 2:9

David Wells writes, "The fundamental problem in the evangelical world today is not inadequate technique...it is that God rests too inconsequentially upon the church. His truth is too distant, his grace too ordinary...and his Christ too common."

This results in failing to view salvation as God's miraculous work, for which we don't receive credit. We must never get over the grace of Jesus. Any day we lose sight of the gospel of grace is a dark day.

Philip Yancey says, "Grace is the most perplexing, powerful force in the universe, and, I believe, the only hope for our twisted, violent planet."

> "A gospel that gets your sins forgiven but offers
> no power for transformation is too small."
>
> **Fred Sanders**

DAY 117

*Do not love the world or anything in the
world. If anyone loves the world, love
for the Father is not in them.*

1 JOHN 2:15

We're to love the world (its people for whom Christ died) in the way our gracious God loves it, but we're to hate the world (its sin and rebellion against God) the way he hates it. Hence, the way we best love the world (people) is by not loving the world (sin). By his grace we see him for who he is and sin for what it is. We're compelled to run toward him and away from sin.

> "You and I have need of the strongest spell that can be found to wake us from the evil enchantment of worldliness."
>
> **C.S. Lewis**

DAY 118

In keeping with his promise we are looking forward to a new heaven and a new earth, where righteousness dwells.

2 Peter 3:13

We get tired of ourselves, of others, of sin and suffering. Yet we love the earth, don't we? I love the spaciousness of the night sky. I love the coziness of sitting next to Nanci on the couch, blanket over us and our golden retriever Maggie snuggled next to us. These experiences aren't Heaven—but they're foretastes of Heaven, a New Earth where we'll behold the greatness of Christ and endlessly enjoy the derivative goodness of his grace and kindness.

"Joy to the world the Lord is come;
Let earth receive her King."

Isaac Watts

DAY 119

Come to me, all you who are weary and burdened,
and I will give you rest. Take my yoke upon you
and learn from me, for I am gentle and humble
in heart, and you will find rest for your souls.
For my yoke is easy and my burden is light.

MATTHEW 11:28-30

In moments of pride, we need to fear God and repent. In moments of despair, we need to just bathe in his grace, and see his smile and hear him say, "Enter into your Master's happiness."

> "Let us but feel that he has his heart set upon us,
> that he is watching us from those heavens with
> tender interest...that he has set his love upon
> us, and in spite of ourselves is working out for
> us his higher will and blessing, as far as we will
> let him—and then nothing can discourage us."
>
> **A.B. Simpson**

DAY 120

It is God's will that you should be sanctified:
that you should avoid sexual immorality; that
each of you should learn to control your own
body in a way that is holy and honorable.

1 THESSALONIANS 4:3-4

Our sexual struggles should remind us of our need for grace and strength—and make us long for our ultimate redemption. If a lifetime of purity seems inconceivable to you, commit yourself in twenty-four-hour increments. Today, "run away from sexual sin" (1 Corinthians 6:18 ERV). Do you want freedom from the actions and obsessions of lust? Get help. Be wise. Avoid temptation. Go to Christ. Experience the sufficiency of his grace. Draw on his power.

> "Christians don't flirt with sexual
> immorality. They flee from it."
>
> **Kevin DeYoung**

DAY 121

No longer will there be any curse. The throne of God and of the Lamb will be in the city, and his servants will serve him.

REVELATION 22:3

Thank you, King Jesus, for paying an unspeakable price to redeem us, in which you became "a curse for us" (Galatians 3:13). For now, this world still writhes under the curse. Meanwhile we trust that while still living in a world that's marred and groaning, wherever the will of God shall lead us, the grace of God shall keep us. Remind us daily of your promise that in Christ the curse will be forever reversed.

"Permit Your unseen servants to be ever active on my behalf, and to rejoice when grace expands in me. Suffer them never to rest until my conflict is over, and I stand victorious on salvation's shore."

Puritan Prayer

DAY 122

Whoever conceals their sins does not prosper,
but the one who confesses and
renounces them finds mercy.

PROVERBS 28:13

We should keep short accounts with God. When we sin, we should confess immediately, relying on God's grace and mercy for forgiveness. Otherwise, we'll become desensitized and go another step further before our dulled conscience objects. Delayed confession is the next worst thing to no confession.

Confession that doesn't show itself in ongoing repentance rings hollow. Thomas Watson said, "Repentance is a grace of God's Spirit whereby a sinner is inwardly humbled and visibly reformed."

> "The way to cover our sin is to
> uncover it by confession."
>
> **Richard Sibbes**

DAY 123

*This same Good News that came to you is going out
all over the world. It is bearing fruit everywhere
by changing lives, just as it changed your lives
from the day you first heard and understood
the truth about God's wonderful grace.*

COLOSSIANS 1:6 (NLT)

Attempts to soften the gospel by minimizing truth keep people from Jesus. Attempts to toughen the gospel by minimizing grace keep people from Jesus. It's not enough for us to offer grace or truth. We must lovingly offer both. John Owen said, "Evangelical truth will not be honourably witnessed unto but by evangelical grace."

"If we don't demonstrate grace as we present the
truth of Jesus Christ, we make the message we
are carrying undesirable and nondistinctive."

Ravi Zacharias

DAY 124

*Dear friends, let us love one another, for
love comes from God. Everyone who loves
has been born of God and knows God.*

1 JOHN 4:7

Thank you, Lord, for using the dark backdrop of my sin
and the emptiness of my heart to enhance the brightness of
your redeeming grace. I've been forgiven much; empower
me now to love much. Keep me from looking at others and
then congratulating myself for my own virtue, when my
sins may simply be different from theirs.

Puritan Thomas Brooks wrote, "It is sad to consider
that saints should have many eyes to behold one another's infirmities, and not one eye to see each other's graces."

Lord, may I love with a love like yours and from yours:
overflowing, spilling over onto those around me.

> "The thing that awakens the deepest
> well of gratitude in a human being
> is that God has forgiven sin."
>
> **Oswald Chambers**

DAY 125

After this I heard what sounded like the roar of a great multitude in heaven shouting: "Hallelujah! Salvation and glory and power belong to our God."

REVELATION 19:1

Lord, every joy Heaven offers is derivative of you, who are joy itself. Heaven will be a grace-filled, thrilling adventure because you're a grace-filled, thrilling person. You said of the New Earth that you'll make for your resurrected people, "Look! God's dwelling place is now among the people, and he will dwell with them" (Revelation 21:3). Thanks for being the source of all great adventures, including those awaiting us in the new universe. I can hardly wait!

> "Heaven...the greatest wonder of all will be to find ourselves there! I am sure that everyone...feels it to be a marvel and he or she resolves, 'If I am saved, I will sing the loudest of them all, for I shall owe most to the abounding mercy of God!'"
>
> Charles Spurgeon

DAY 126

*And we know that in all things God works
for the good of those who love him, who
have been called according to his purpose.*

ROMANS 8:28

As Christians, we are not immune to the curse, but even the very bad in life is part of the "all things" God will ultimately work together for our good. We are sustained through great heartache by knowing we're strengthened by God's Spirit, covered by his grace, and assured of the resurrection.

Timothy Keller summarizes Romans 8:28-30 this way: "Your bad things will turn out for good, your good things can never be lost, and your best things are yet to come."

"People treat God's sovereignty as a
matter of controversy, but in Scripture
it is a matter of worship."

J.I. Packer

DAY 127

*There is rejoicing in the presence of the angels
of God over one sinner who repents.*

LUKE 15:10

Those in Heaven see and celebrate conversions on Earth. Sinners embracing God's grace means it's party time in Heaven. And it should mean party time on Earth.

As Greg Laurie says, "True repentance will always lead to true rejoicing, for biblical repentance always leads to believing and clinging to the gospel—the good news for repentant sinners."

Let's make sure we rejoice concerning what all Heaven— God and his angels and his people—are rejoicing about.

> "If heaven were by merit, it would never be
> heaven to me, for...I should say, 'I am sure I
> am here by mistake; I am sure this is not my
> place...' But if it be of grace and not of works,
> then we may walk into heaven with boldness."
>
> Charles Spurgeon

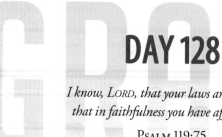

DAY 128

I know, LORD, that your laws are righteous,
that in faithfulness you have afflicted me.

PSALM 119:75

If you're experiencing disease, broken relationships, or other afflictions, you may think, *I refuse to accept that my suffering can prove worthwhile.* But God says, "this light momentary affliction is preparing for us an eternal weight of glory beyond all comparison" (2 Corinthians 4:17 ESV).

Rejecting God's goodness will not make you better or happier; it will only bring resentment and greater pain. Accept health as God's gracious blessing and its absence as God's severe mercy. He's still on the throne, and whether in this life or the next, he *will* grant you the longings of your heart.

> "Our little time of suffering is not worthy of our first night's welcome home to Heaven."
>
> **Samuel Rutherford**

DAY 129

In him and through faith in him we may
approach God with freedom and confidence.

EPHESIANS 3:12

We can come to Jesus freely and confidently. He has never sinned, but he is able to "empathize with our weaknesses" (Hebrews 4:15).

J. Gresham Machen wrote, "The very center and core of the whole Bible is the doctrine of the grace of God...The theologians of the Church can be placed in an ascending scale according as they have grasped that one great central doctrine...The center of the Bible, and the center of Christianity, is found in the grace of God."

It's true: "The LORD is compassionate and gracious, slow to anger, abounding in love" (Psalm 103:8).

> "Jesus' death is your guarantee that when
> you come to God and confess your
> sins to him, you will receive mercy."

David Powlison

DAY 130

Like the rest, we were by nature deserving of wrath.

EPHESIANS 2:3

My sins and yours nailed Jesus to that cross as surely as the sins of a child killer or the terrorist who flew a 767 into a World Trade Center tower. Only the incomparable riches of God's grace could deliver us. The cost of redemption cannot be overstated. The wonders of grace cannot be over-emphasized. Christ left Heaven and took upon himself the Hell we deserved, so we could have the Heaven we don't deserve.

> "A Substitute has appeared, appointed by God himself, to bear the weight and the burden of our transgressions, to make expiation for our guilt, and to propitiate the wrath of God on our behalf. This is the gospel."
>
> **R.C. Sproul**

DAY 131

*If, while we were God's enemies, we were
reconciled to him through the death of his
Son, how much more, having been reconciled,
shall we be saved through his life!*

Romans 5:10

It's only through the atoning work of Christ that any of us
will be in Heaven, but we might be surprised about some
we see there and some we don't. And perhaps we'll find it
most amazing of all that we are there—we who deserve
Hell but have been given Heaven because of what Jesus did
on the cross. What magnificent grace!

> "In the unimaginable wonder of his grace,
> he himself grasped that fiery sword of
> wrath, plunged it at the cross into his
> own heart, and extinguished it there. He
> did this for us, foolish, sinning rebels."
>
> Bruce Milne

DAY 132

He who was seated on the throne said, "I am making everything new!" Then he said, "Write this down, for these words are trustworthy and true."

REVELATION 21:5

We can take Christ's words to the bank. His promises are secured by his blood. To those who've experienced and are experiencing tragic loss, suffering, and illness—may the God of all grace encourage your hearts as you look forward to the day when all will be made new and right and forever wonderful.

"He that rides to be crowned, will not think much of a rainy day."

John Trapp

DAY 133

It is by grace you have been saved, through faith—
and this is not from yourselves, it is the gift of
God—not by works, so that no one can boast.

Ephesians 2:8

Martyn Lloyd-Jones said, "If you think you deserve heaven, take it from me, you are not a Christian." That may sound harsh, but it's simply true.

If you're waiting until you become worthy of God's grace, don't hold your breath. If we deserved it we wouldn't need it. The beauty is that though God sees us at our worst, he still eagerly and freely extends to us his grace in Christ.

Despite our complete unworthiness, he offers us the gift of eternal life, based on his death for our sins on the cross. Rejoice! Burk Parsons says, "There is more grace in Christ than sin in you."

> "Man is born broken. He lives by
> mending. The grace of God is glue."
> **Eugene Gladstone O'Neill**

DAY 134

The love of money is a root of all kinds of evil.
Some people, eager for money, have wandered from
the faith and pierced themselves with many griefs.

1 Timothy 6:10

The only way to survive prosperity is, by God's grace, to view money and possessions as gifts from his gracious hand, and to use them generously to help others.

Giving is the only way to break the back of materialism: "Command those who are rich in this present world not to be arrogant nor to put their hope in wealth, which is so uncertain, but to put their hope in God, who richly provides us with everything for our enjoyment. Command them to do good, to be rich in good deeds, and to be generous and willing to share" (1 Timothy 6:17-18).

> "The world asks, 'What does a man own?
> 'Christ asks, 'How does he use it?'"
>
> Andrew Murray

DAY 135

Whoever sows sparingly will also reap sparingly,
and whoever sows generously will also reap
generously. Each of you should give what you have
decided in your heart to give, not reluctantly or
under compulsion, for God loves a cheerful giver.

2 CORINTHIANS 9:6-7

Our giving is a reflexive response to the grace of God in our lives. It doesn't come out of our unselfishness or philanthropy—it comes out of the transforming work of Christ in us. Those who know their need seize grace as a hungry man seizes bread. Upon realizing he has discovered the bakery, he throws open the doors and invites others to join the feast!

> "The less I spent on myself and the more
> I gave to others, the fuller of happiness
> and blessing did my soul become."
>
> **Hudson Taylor**

DAY 136

Then Jesus said to his disciples, "Whoever wants to be my disciple must deny themselves and take up their cross and follow me."

MATTHEW 16:24

While a Christian should maintain high moral standards, many believers fail to recognize that such standards are insufficient. They're not inherently life-changing. We must always go back to the cross, to the gospel and grace of Christ. They can generate a moral life, but a moral life cannot generate them.

> "Holiness is not attained, at least not in any lasting, life-changing way, merely through prohibitions, threats, fear, or shame-based appeals. Holiness is attained by believing in, trusting, banking on, resting in, savoring, and cherishing God's promise of a superior happiness that comes only by falling in love with Jesus."
>
> Sam Storms

DAY 137

*I will sprinkle clean water on you, and you
will be clean; I will cleanse you from all your
impurities and from all your idols. I will give
you a new heart and put a new spirit in you.*

EZEKIEL 36:25-26

If you think your sin is greater than God's grace and strength, you're disbelieving the promises of God. You are greatly underestimating the power of God. And in doing so you are greatly overestimating yourself. There is great freedom in recognizing both God's infinite greatness and our finite smallness.

"When it is a question of God's
almighty Spirit, never say, 'I can't.'"

Oswald Chambers

DAY 138

[The grace of God] teaches us to say "No"
to ungodliness and worldly passions, and
to live self-controlled, upright and
godly lives in this present age.

Titus 2:12

Some act as if God's grace means sin doesn't matter, or it's inevitable that we always keep falling. God's grace not only forgives our sin, it empowers us to live in holiness. Grace is not just what saved us once; it's what saves us every day. D.L. Moody said, "The law tells me how crooked I am. Grace comes along and straightens me out."

"What is sin?
It is the glory of God not honored.
The holiness of God not reverenced...
The faithfulness of God not trusted.
The commandments of God not obeyed.
The justice of God not respected.
The wrath of God not feared.
The grace of God not cherished."

John Piper

DAY 139

May the God of hope fill you with all joy and peace
as you trust in him, so that you may overflow
with hope by the power of the Holy Spirit.

ROMANS 15:13

A.W. Tozer wrote, "Abounding sin is the terror of the world, but abounding grace is the hope of mankind."

In a world of sin and suffering, where is our hope but in God's grace? When we live with eternity in mind, it infuses us with a joy that sustains us in our daily life, even as we face difficulties. Sometimes the greater the difficulties, the more we're brought to the end of ourselves. Then we recognize what's always true even when we don't realize it: we are utterly insufficient, while his grace is utterly sufficient.

> "What is your hope? Only this—his relentless grace, boundless love, patient forgiveness, and unending faithfulness."
>
> Paul Tripp

DAY 140

Consider it pure joy, my brothers and sisters,
whenever you face trials of many kinds,
because you know that the testing of your
faith produces perseverance. Let perseverance
finish its work so that you may be mature
and complete, not lacking anything.

JAMES 1:2-4

The assumption that life shouldn't be so hard leads to self-pity and endless finger-pointing. We see life as unfair and ourselves as victims, and focus on the offenses others have done. We don't realize they pale in comparison to our own offenses against God, who through his grace not only forgives us, but requires and enables us to forgive others and move forward in freedom.

> "Pain isn't for God's benefit; he uses it
> for ours. He is a God who redeems. It
> hurts to straighten what is bent."
>
> **Julia Stager Mayo**

DAY 141

Those who belong to Christ Jesus have crucified the flesh with its passions and desires.

GALATIANS 5:24

The greater our grasp of our sin and alienation from God, the greater our grasp of God's grace. The more we love grace, the more we want to put sin to death. Greg Laurie says, "Remorse for sin is sour, but it leads to the sweetness of the gospel."

The more we recognize our helplessness to rescue ourselves, the more heroic and indispensable we recognize God's rescue of us really is. And the more we will love him for it.

"Till sin be bitter, Christ will not be sweet."

Thomas Watson

DAY 142

*Therefore, since we have been justified
by faith, we have peace with God
through our Lord Jesus Christ.*

ROMANS 5:1

Life under the curse is hard. (That's why it's called the curse!) Instead of complaining about everything that goes wrong, let's thank God that he in his kindness has given us not only a wide variety of favorable circumstances, but peace and deliverance, grace and eternal life. God rejoices in the grace he offers us and he rejoices at our joy in receiving it.

> "Would you know who is the greatest saint in the world? It is not he who prays the most or fasts the most, it is not he who lives the most, but it is he who is always thankful to God, who receives everything as an instance of God's goodness and has a heart always ready to praise God for it."

> **William Law**

DAY 143

*Carrying his own cross, he went out to the
place of the Skull... There they crucified him.*

JOHN 19:17-18

What's good about Good Friday? Since the crucifixion of
Jesus was the greatest injustice of human history, why isn't
it called Bad Friday? Because out of the appallingly bad
came what was inexpressibly good. And the good trumps
the bad because the bad was temporary while the good is
eternal. God's love and grace come to us soaked in divine
blood.

> "'My will, not thine, be done,' changed Paradise
> into a desert; 'Thy will, not mine, be done,'
> changed the desert back again into Paradise."
>
> **James Campbell**

DAY 144

All of you clothe yourselves with humility
toward one another, because
"God resists the proud
but gives grace to the humble."

1 Peter 5:5 (hcsb)

Humility preserves us; pride destroys us. This means acting in arrogance is like wearing a sign before God that says "go ahead and resist me." That's a prayer he's certain to answer. Every day, every hour, we choose either to humble ourselves or to be proud. Humility wears the sign "give me grace," a prayer God is always happy to answer.

> "[The humble person] will not be
> thinking about humility; he will not
> be thinking about himself at all."
>
> C.S. Lewis

DAY 145

Whom have I in heaven but you?
And earth has nothing I desire besides you.

PSALM 73:25

God's greatest gift is himself. We don't need just salvation; we need Jesus, the Savior. It's the person, God, who graciously offers us the place, Heaven, a place purchased by his blood. Near the end of his life, John Newton said, "Although my memory's fading, I remember two things very clearly: I am a great sinner and Christ is a great Savior."

"I am born for God only. Christ is nearer to me than father, or mother, or sister—a near relation, a more affectionate Friend; and I rejoice to follow him, and to love him."

Henry Martyn

DAY 146

Yet the LORD longs to be gracious to you;
therefore he will rise up to show you compassion.
For the LORD is a God of justice.
Blessed are all who wait for him!

ISAIAH 30:18

Faith means believing that God is good. Even if we can't see it today, one day we'll look back and see clearly his goodness and kindness and grace. Countless believers have attested to this truth as they neared the end of their difficult lives. All God's children will know it one day. May we not wait until then to learn it is true!

> "I have learned that faith means trusting in advance what will only make sense in reverse."
>
> **Philip Yancey**

DAY 147

*Dear friends, now we are children of God, and
what we will be has not yet been made known.
But we know that when Christ appears, we
shall be like him, for we shall see him as he is.*

1 John 3:2

In Heaven, we won't gaze into the mirror wishing for different physical features. The sinless beauty of the inner person will overflow into the beauty of the outer person. We'll feel neither insecure nor arrogant. We'll know that the Artist fashioned us just as he desired and that we'll never lose the health and beauty he's graciously given us.

> "To be begotten is something more than to be made; this is a more personal work of God, and that which is begotten is in closer affinity to him than that which is only created."

Charles Spurgeon

DAY 148

He has shown kindness by giving you rain from heaven and crops in their seasons; he provides you with plenty of food and fills your hearts with joy.

ACTS 14:17

Paul was speaking here to unbelievers. Don't evil and suffering grab everyone's attention precisely because they seem wrong and out of place? We "get the flu" because we normally don't have it. We break an arm that usually remains unbroken. Our shock at evil testifies to the predominance of good. Though fallen, nature still contains more beauty than ugliness.

By God's common grace, believers and unbelievers alike see considerable and remarkable good in the world. It should remind God's children of Paradise and point us toward the New Earth—which can be ours only by his saving grace.

"All beauty in the world is either a memory of Paradise or a prophecy of the transfigured world."

Nicholas Berdyaev

DAY 149

Do your best to come to me quickly, for Demas, because he loved this world, has deserted me and has gone to Thessalonica.

2 TIMOTHY 4:9-10

Those in love with this world never get the best it has to offer. They're forever disillusioned. Christian pilgrims have no such illusions. They appreciate the world for what it is—a magnificent creation of a most gracious God who alone can fill the emptiness of their heart. But they never imagine that when the world promises freedom, it speaks the truth.

Charles Swindoll writes, "Grace is ours. Let's live it! Deny it or debate it and we kill it. My plea is that we claim it and allow it to set us free."

> "Because we love something else more than this world, we love even this world better than those who know no other."
>
> C.S. Lewis

DAY 150

He has made everything beautiful in its time. He has also set eternity in the human heart; yet no one can fathom what God has done from beginning to end.

<small>ECCLESIASTES 3:11</small>

Think about particular spiritual moments you've experienced—perhaps in prayer, a conversation with a loved one, gazing up into the bright stars of a night sky. Have you ever had a sense of moving on the edge of eternity, catching a faint glimpse of what the universe is about? This was just a sneak peek, the awakening of a desire that lies deep within, where God by his grace has set eternity in our hearts.

> "[The Christian] is now new-born, and becomes a child of eternity; whereby his heart is fallen in love with new and everlasting delights, and the eye of his soul turned from the dung of this world towards the glory of the second life."
>
> **Robert Bolton**

DAY 151

My Father's house has many rooms;
if that were not so, would I have told you that
I am going there to prepare a place for you?...
I will come back and take you to be with me
that you also may be where I am.

JOHN 14:2-3

Like a bride's dreams of sharing a home with her groom, our love for Heaven should be overflowing and contagious, like our love for God. The more I learn about our gracious God, the more excited I get about Heaven. The more I learn about Heaven, the more excited I get about God.

> "The Bride eyes not her garment,
> But her dear Bridegroom's face;
> I will not gaze at glory,
> But on my King of grace;
> Not on the crown He giveth,
> But on His pierced hand:
> The Lamb is all the glory
> Of Immanuel's land."

Anne Ross Cousin

DAY 152

*For our light and momentary troubles
are achieving for us an eternal glory
that far outweighs them all.*

2 Corinthians 4:17

G.K. Chesterton's fictional character, Father Brown, said, "We are on the wrong side of the tapestry." How true. We see the knots and the snarls underneath. But God is on the right side of the tapestry, weaving it by his grace into a beautiful work of art. We may not always know what the Master Artist is doing in our lives. But he does—and that's far more important.

> "What we judge to be 'tragic—the most dreaded thing that could happen,' I expect we'll one day see as the awesome reason for the beauty and uniqueness of our life and our family."
>
> Elisabeth Elliot

DAY 153

*Surely God does not reject one who is blameless
or strengthen the hands of evildoers.
He will yet fill your mouth with laughter
and your lips with shouts of joy.*

Job 8:20-21

Often we think of ourselves as fun-loving, and of God as a humorless killjoy. But we've got it backward. It's not God who's boring; it's us. Did we invent wit, humor, and laughter? No. God did. Thank him today for his promise to fill your mouth with laughter. Regard humor and laughter as his gracious gifts that flow freely from the deep riches of his happiness.

> "God is the only source of real happiness. He does not need anything or anyone to make him happy: even before he made the world, the three persons of the Trinity were completely happy with each other. What God does for Christians is to make them as happy as he is."
>
> Jeremiah Burroughs

DAY 154

As a father has compassion on his children,
so the LORD has compassion on those who fear him.

PSALM 103:13

God is the source of all good and the standard by which it's measured. We may not like all that God does, but we're in no position to accuse him of wrongdoing. Every breath he gives us is a gracious gift. And as David reminds us, his compassion is like that of a father toward his children. The children often don't know best, but the Father always does.

> "[God is] with us when the sun is shining, but
> we've got to remember he's still beside us
> when it's raining. He understands the pain
> you're enduring more than you'll ever know.
> And when your tears are dried and the trial is
> past? You'll see that Jesus was in it all along.
> It's what a compassionate God does."

Joni Eareckson Tada

DAY 155

To me, to live is Christ and to die is gain.

PHILIPPIANS 1:21

By God's grace, death for the Christian is not the end of adventure but the doorway to a world where dreams and adventures forever expand. No matter how bad the present, an eternity with Christ in Heaven will be incomparably better. So if God thinks the whole thing is worth it—and we know it will be to us once we reach Heaven—then why not affirm by faith, even in the midst of suffering, that it's worth it now?

> "That is what mortals misunderstand. They say of some temporal suffering, 'No future bliss can make up for it' not knowing that Heaven, once attained, will work backwards and turn even that agony into a glory."

> C.S. Lewis

DAY 156

Since we have now been justified by his
blood, how much more shall we be saved
from God's wrath through him!

ROMANS 5:9

If you feel angry at God, what price would you have him pay for his "failure" to do more for people facing suffering and evil? Would you inflict capital punishment on him? You're too late. He already imposed that on himself, willingly dying for us. No matter how bitter we feel toward God, could any of us come up with a punishment worse than what God in his grace chose to take upon himself for us? Not because he deserved it, but because we did!

> "God's wrath against sin was unleashed in all its
> fury on his beloved Son. He held nothing back."
>
> Jerry Bridges

DAY 157

But we do see Jesus, who was made lower than the angels for a little while, now crowned with glory and honor because he suffered death, so that by the grace of God he might taste death for everyone.

HEBREWS 2:9

It's one thing to suffer terribly, another to *choose*, eyes wide open, to suffer terribly. Evil and suffering formed the crucible in which God demonstrated his grace and love to mankind. He didn't have to die for us. He did so, knowing in advance the unspeakable agony, fully comprehending the incredible cost. What unstoppable love. What amazing grace!

> "One short glimpse, one transitory vision of his glory, one brief glance at his marred, but now exalted and beaming countenance, would repay almost a world of trouble."
>
> Charles Spurgeon

DAY 158

*We know that the whole creation
has been groaning as in the pains of
childbirth...We ourselves...groan inwardly
as we wait eagerly for our adoption to
sonship, the redemption of our bodies.*

ROMANS 8:22-23

The goodness we see now is but a whiff of Mama's stew—a hint of the feast awaiting us. We see only marred remnants of Eden. If the "wrong side" of Heaven can look beautiful, what will the "right side" look like? What will Earth look like when God makes it new?

"When you and I come to lie upon our death beds, the one thing that should comfort and help and strengthen us there is the thing that helped us in the beginning...Not what we have been, not what we have done, but the grace of God in Jesus Christ our Lord. The Christian life starts with grace, it must continue with grace, it ends with grace."

Martyn Lloyd-Jones

DAY 159

Your Father knows what you
need before you ask him.

MATTHEW 6:8

God is gracious and good and sits on the throne of the universe, and everything that comes into our lives is Father-filtered. So how can we be pessimistic? The Christian's optimism is based squarely on realism: God is real, the atonement is real, the resurrection is real, the second coming is real, God's providence is real, and the gospel really is "good news."

> "Whatsoever is good for God's children they shall have it; for all is theirs to help them towards heaven; therefore if poverty be good they shall have it; if disgrace or crosses be good they shall have them; for all is ours to promote our greatest prosperity."
>
> **Richard Sibbes**

DAY 160

That's why we can be so sure that every detail in our lives of love for God is worked into something good.

ROMANS 8:28 (MSG)

I believe that if God in his grace could not use something, in eternity, to contribute to the good of his child, then he will not permit it to happen. Paul doesn't say that God causes some or most things to work for our good, but *all* things, "every detail."

Charles Swindoll says, "Believing in grace is one thing. Living it is another." We can live it only when we come to terms with the trustworthiness of God's promise that he loves us so much he will truly work *all things* for our good.

> "The true original and prime motive of all gracious, bountiful expressions and effusions of love upon [God's] elect, is the good pleasure of his will."
>
> Robert Bolton

DAY 161

The LORD is my rock, my fortress and my deliverer;
my God is my rock, in whom I take refuge,
my shield and the horn of my
salvation, my stronghold.

PSALM 18:2

None of us is more secure than the object of our trust. If our trust is in material things—a house, a certain job, or people—we set ourselves up to worry. Those things are unreliable. God isn't, and he graciously invites us to make him our stronghold. "Command those who are rich in this present world not to be arrogant nor to put their hope in wealth, which is so uncertain, but to put their hope in God" (1 Timothy 6:17).

"Trusting God does not mean believing that he will do all that you want, but rather believing that he will do everything he knows is good."

Ken Sande

DAY 162

Cast all your anxiety on him
because he cares for you.

1 PETER 5:7

Who is this "he" who cares for you? The God who loved
you so much to go to the cross for you, who has seen you
at your very worst and still lavished his grace upon you.
The kind-hearted God for whom you need not perform or
achieve, just be. The God who knows all, governs all, and
weaves all together for your good and his glory.

> "The greatest sorrow and burden you can lay
> upon the Father, the greatest unkindness you
> can do to him, is not to believe that he loves you."
>
> John Owen

DAY 163

Sovereign LORD, you have begun to show to your servant your greatness and your strong hand. For what god is there in heaven or on earth who can do the deeds and mighty works you do?

DEUTERONOMY 3:24

Timothy Keller says, "Why does God have to punish sin? Because he's so good. Why does God want to forgive sin? Because he's so good."

In this life we can only begin to see God's goodness and greatness—but it's vital that we do. When we're with him, we'll know it was worth it to have lived in this world of sin and suffering. The grace of Jesus changes everything—including you and me.

"Since God is infinite, and in him are all treasures of wisdom, we would throughout eternity be ever searching, ever learning, yet would never exhaust the riches of his wisdom, his goodness, or his power."

Walton Brown

He knows the way I take;
When He has tried me, I shall come forth as gold.
My foot has held fast to His path;
I have kept His way and not turned aside.
I have not departed from the command of His lips;
I have treasured the words of His mouth
more than my necessary food.

JOB 23:10-12 (NASB)

For God's child, there is no pointless suffering. Much of it may appear pointless, since finite fallen creatures are incapable of understanding the point. But our gracious God is all-wise and all-loving and never pointless nor off point. That's why Job could cry out in agony, "Though he slay me, yet will I hope in him" (Job 13:15).

> "God whispers to us in our pleasures, speaks
> in our consciences, but shouts in our pains.
> It is his megaphone to rouse a deaf world."
>
> **C.S. Lewis**

DAY 165

*All Scripture is God-breathed and is
useful for teaching, rebuking, correcting
and training in righteousness.*

2 TIMOTHY 3:16

If I would listen to the voice of the Spirit, I should "put my ear" to the Word of God. Why wait for the Spirit to speak when I have in my hands what he has graciously already spoken? The question is, am I listening? And if I don't hear what I want to, will I continue to listen anyway?

> "The vigor of our spiritual life will be in exact proportion to the place held by the Bible in our life and thoughts."
>
> **George Müller**

DAY 166

See, I will create
new heavens and a new earth.
The former things will not be remembered,
nor will they come to mind.

Isaiah 65:17

Without Christ, both Earth and mankind would be doomed. But Christ came, died, and rose from the grave. He brought deliverance, not destruction. Ray Ortlund says, "He came down from God as the archetypal new man, our better self, our only future." Because of the grace of Christ, we are not doomed, and neither is the Earth.

By far the best is yet to come!

> "Our Lord has written the promise of
> the resurrection not in books alone,
> but in every leaf in spring-time."
>
> **Martin Luther**

DAY 167

The Spirit you received does not make you slaves,
so that you live in fear again; rather, the Spirit
you received brought about your adoption to
sonship. And by him we cry, "Abba, Father."

ROMANS 8:15

In many Scripture passages, God calls upon us to fear him. But once our sins are confessed he graciously says we can come to him saying, "*Abba*, Father," meaning Papa or Daddy. We can come confidently before his throne with the access permitted only to the King's children. We still fear him, but in a way that does not diminish our love for him or his for us.

> "The first person of the Trinity has many names—
> Almighty One, Creator, Most High, Holy Holy Holy,
> the Rock, the Great I Am. But when Jesus came
> to tear away the veil so we could look directly
> into the heart of God, he revealed God as 'Father.'"
>
> Mary Kassian

DAY 168

Our citizenship is in heaven.
And we eagerly await a Savior from there,
the Lord Jesus Christ,
who, by the power that enables him to
bring everything under his control,
will transform our lowly bodies so that
they will be like his glorious body.

Philippians 3:20-21

I believe that in the eternal Heaven centered on the New Earth, reading and study and discussion, and all forms of intellectual exploration, will not only still exist but be greatly enriched. We will remain God's image-bearers, fully human, but we will be at last unhindered by sin. Learning more of God and his universe will be a constant pleasure, untainted by error or arrogance, infused by his grace.

> "The Christian is the really free man—he is free to have imagination. This too is our heritage. The Christian is the one whose imagination should fly beyond the stars."

> **Francis Schaeffer**

DAY 169

*May our Lord Jesus Christ himself and God
our Father, who loved us and by his grace
gave us eternal encouragement and good
hope, encourage your hearts and strengthen
you in every good deed and word.*

2 THESSALONIANS 2:16-17

Giving, and other good deeds, are a subset of God's grace.
We love because he first loved us, we give because he first
gave to us. We give back to God because he first gave to us.
As we enter into his generosity, we enter into his happiness,
his purpose and plan. We break free from the money and
things that hold us in bondage.

> "A true faith in Jesus Christ will not suffer us
> to be idle. No, it is an active, lively, restless
> principle; it fills the heart, so that it cannot be
> easy till it is doing something for Jesus Christ."

George Whitefield

DAY 170

Having been justified by his grace, we might become heirs having the hope of eternal life.

TITUS 3:7

Our God is a God of joy-filled surprises. The greatest surprise is also the greatest certainty: his grace. I do not doubt for a moment I will be in Heaven. For it is dependent on him, not on me. I thank him for his assurance that what he has done for me is far greater than what I have done against him. If it depended on me, I would have no hope. Because it depends on Jesus, I have nothing but hope.

> "For we are not saved by believing in our own salvation, nor by believing anything whatsoever about ourselves. We are saved by what we believe about the Son of God and his righteousness. The gospel believed saves; not the believing in our own faith."
>
> **Horatius Bonar**

DAY 171

Instead, speaking the truth in love, we will grow to become in every respect the mature body of him who is the head, that is, Christ.

EPHESIANS 4:15

Unfortunately, many nonbelievers know only two kinds of Christians: those who speak truth without grace and those who are gracious but never share the truth. What they need to see is a third kind—who, in a humble spirit of grace, love them enough to tell the truth...as cheerfully as possible. Isaac Newton said, "Tact is the art of making a point without making an enemy."

> "A cheerful, kindly spirit is a great recommendation to a believer. It is a positive misfortune to Christianity when a Christian cannot smile. A merry heart, and a readiness to take part in all innocent mirth, are gifts of inestimable value. They go far to soften prejudices...and to make way for Christ and the gospel."
>
> **J.C. Ryle**

DAY 172

*Do not rejoice that the spirits submit to you, but
rejoice that your names are written in heaven.*

LUKE 10:20

We should rejoice in God's accomplishments more than ours. If we can begin to grasp God's grace for us, if we fall on our knees and weep, and then if we dance and smile and shout and laugh out loud because God has overwhelmed us with his grace, people will see Jesus in us. They will believe what we tell them about Jesus, because we—just like him— will be full of grace. Just as our grouchiness will drive people from the gospel, our happiness in him will draw them to the gospel.

> "Sin is Hell, grace is Heaven; what madness
> it is to look more at Hell than Heaven."
>
> **Thomas Brooks**

DAY 173

I consider my life worth nothing to me; my only aim is to finish the race and complete the task the Lord Jesus has given me—the task of testifying to the good news of God's grace.

ACTS 20:24

The gospel is not good advice; it's good news. It delivers us from sin and misery. We've been entrusted with a message of incalculable value. All people crave happiness and the gospel is called "the good news of happiness" (Isaiah 52:7 ESV). Since it's the most worthy message in the universe and we—with all our inadequacy—are the chosen message-bearers, we should eagerly learn to convey it more effectively.

> "We do not fail in our evangelism if we faithfully tell the gospel to someone who is not subsequently converted; we fail only if we do not faithfully tell the gospel at all."

Mark Dever

DAY 174

Now that you have been set free from sin and have become slaves of God, the benefit you reap leads to holiness, and the result is eternal life.

ROMANS 6:22

If you have come to Christ, God says that by his grace you have been "set free from sin." He has taken off the shackles and unlocked the door. Truly. You are free! But you have to choose to walk out of the cell and live the free life. That's when your freedom becomes not theoretical but real.

> "The gospel of grace is a message of breathtaking freedom...You are thoroughly accepted just as you are. Jesus Christ is your righteousness and he is never going to change...Your spirit needs to bask in the brilliant sunlight of this reality."
>
> **Terry Virgo**

DAY 175

Give thanks to the LORD, for he is good;
his love endures forever.

PSALM 107:1

God's goodness is always evident if we look in the right place. "He is not far from any one of us. 'For in him we live and move and have our being'" (Acts 17:27-28).

Thank you, dear Lord, for your grace and kindness to us all. Remind us to celebrate all that you have done for us—the big things, such as election and redemption, and the thousands of little things that surround us every minute of every day.

> "Grace isn't a little prayer you chant before
> receiving a meal. It's a way to live."
>
> **D.L. Moody**

DAY 176

May all who seek you
rejoice and be glad in you!
May those who love your salvation
say evermore, "God is great!"

Psalm 70:4 (esv)

C.S. Lewis said, "Grace substitutes a full, childlike and delighted acceptance of our need, a joy in total dependence. We become 'jolly beggars.'"

We're jolly beggars now, but in the ages to come, we'll be all the more childlike, eagerly learning more about God and his grace, happily discovering more as we forever probe deeper into his attributes.

Don't wait to experience this joy! Put down the phone, turn off the TV, the video games, internet, tablet, and turn your thoughts upon him now. Read his Word and Christ-saturated books that draw you into his presence.

> "I want the presence of God himself, or I don't
> want anything at all to do with religion...
> I want all that God has or I don't want any."
>
> **A.W. Tozer**

DAY 177

Come and see what God has done,
his awesome deeds for mankind!

PSALM 66:5

Can you look at Jesus and not be pierced? Can you see how he loved people and not be broken? Can you hear his words and not thirst for the One who spoke them? Can you gaze on the crucified Christ and still resent God for "not doing enough" to show his love and mercy and grace?

"The other gods were strong, but Thou wast weak;
They rode, but Thou didst stumble to a throne;
But to our wounds only God's wounds can speak,
And not a god has wounds, but Thou alone."

Edward Shillito

DAY 178

The creation was subjected to frustration, not by its own choice, but by the will of the one who subjected it, in hope that the creation itself will be liberated from its bondage to decay and brought into the freedom and glory of the children of God.

ROMANS 8:20-21

The power of Christ's resurrection is infinite—it is enough not only to remake us into the best we could be, but to remake every inch of the universe—mountains, rivers, plants, animals, stars and nebulae and quasars and galaxies. And it's all a result of his abundant grace.

"A person who is obsessed thinks about heaven frequently. Obsessed people orient their lives around eternity; they are not fixed only on what is here in front of them."

Francis Chan

DAY 179

He who did not spare his own Son, but gave him up for us all—how will he not also, along with him, graciously give us all things?

ROMANS 8:32

God is a lavish giver. The God who gave us his Son delights to graciously give us "all things." These things are in addition to Christ, but they are never instead of him—they come "along with him." If we didn't have Christ, we would have nothing. But because we have Christ, we have everything.

"Christians who properly place God as the source and goal of the things they enjoy will find themselves enjoying those things even more."

Steve DeWitt

DAY 180

We do not make requests of you because we are righteous, but because of your great mercy.

DANIEL 9:18

Erwin Lutzer says, "When the mask of self-righteousness has been torn from us and we stand stripped of all our accustomed defenses, we are candidates for God's generous grace."

Our every breath is by God's grace and mercy, not our virtue. What could be more important—and more satisfying—than to set aside time to confess, give thanks to the Lord, recognize his greatness, intercede for others, open his Word, and seek after God?

> "As theology is ultimately the knowledge of God, the more theology I know, the more it should drive me to seek to know God."
>
> **Martyn Lloyd-Jones**

DAY 181

*When you were dead in your sins and in the
uncircumcision of your flesh, God made you alive
with Christ. He forgave us all our sins, having
canceled the charge of our legal indebtedness,
which stood against us and condemned us; he
has taken it away, nailing it to the cross.*

Colossians 2:13-14

The cross was necessary to satisfy God's holy justice, and it graphically demonstrated his love. Peter Kreeft says, "We sinned for no reason but an incomprehensible lack of love, and he saved us for no reason but an incomprehensible excess of love." That "excess of love" is what we call grace.

"The world takes us to a silver screen on which
flickering images of passion and romance play,
and as we watch, the world says, 'This is love.' God
takes us to the foot of a tree on which a naked
and bloodied man hangs and says, 'This is love.'"

Joshua Harris

DAY 182

You intended to harm me, but God intended it for good to accomplish what is now being done, the saving of many lives.

GENESIS 50:20

Henry Francis Lyte wrote, "I need Thy presence ev'ry passing hour. What but Thy grace can foil the tempter's pow'r?"

Jesus said of the devil, "When he lies, he speaks his native language, for he is a liar and the father of lies" (John 8:44). Satan tempts us to doubt God's love and grace. Satan intends your suffering for evil; God intends it for good. Satan attempts to destroy your faith; God invites you to draw upon his sovereign grace to sustain you.

If we recognize God's sovereignty over Satan's work, our perspective isn't merely altered, it's transformed. Our Father's in charge—the devil is *not*!

> "The Lord's mercy often rides to the door of our heart upon the black horse of affliction."
>
> Charles Spurgeon

DAY 183

If anybody does sin, we have an advocate with the Father—Jesus Christ, the Righteous One. He is the atoning sacrifice for our sins.

1 JOHN 2:1-2

As a result of the redemptive work of the Messiah, we're told, "For the accuser of our brothers and sisters, who accuses them before our God day and night, has been hurled down" (Revelation 12:10). Satan is our prosecutor, but his words won't stick. Jesus is both our defense attorney and our judge. A defender and judge who is full of grace!

> "So when the devil throws your sins in your face and declares that you deserve death and hell, tell him this: 'I admit that I deserve death and hell, what of it? For I know One who suffered and made satisfaction on my behalf. His name is Jesus Christ, Son of God, and where he is there I shall be also!'"
>
> **Martin Luther**

DAY 184

*Enter his gates with thanksgiving
and his courts with praise;
give thanks to him and praise his name.*

PSALM 100:4

Cultivating thankfulness today will allow us to cling to God's goodness and grace and mercy in our darkest hours. Those hours lie ahead of us—but beyond them will stretch unending millennia of inexpressible joy that we'll appreciate more deeply because of these fleeting days of darkness. Nancy Leigh DeMoss says, "Undeniable guilt, plus undeserved grace, should equal unbridled gratitude."

> "When we lay the soil of our hard lives open to the rain of grace and let joy penetrate our cracked and dry places, let joy soak into our broken skin and deep crevices, life grows. How can this not be the best thing for the world? For us?"
>
> **Ann Voskamp**

DAY 185

*Those eighteen who died when the tower in Siloam
fell on them—do you think they were more guilty
than all the others living in Jerusalem? I tell you,
no! But unless you repent, you too will all perish.*

Luke 13:4-5

Though God judged individuals and nations in Scripture, we know this *only* because he revealed it. Job's friends wrongly stated God was judging him—but God called Job blameless. We *all* deserve God's judgment; we all live by his grace and mercy. But unlike some people, God will never blame you for what wasn't your fault. And he will forgive you for whatever was. That is grace.

> "Faith dares to fail. The resurrection and the
> judgment will demonstrate before all worlds
> who won and who lost. We can wait."
>
> **A.W. Tozer**

DAY 186

We wait for the blessed hope—the appearing of the glory of our great God and Savior, Jesus Christ.

TITUS 2:13

God is not only gracious and merciful but also all-wise. He knows the right time for each of us to leave this world and the right time to return to set up his kingdom and swallow up death forever. Come, Lord Jesus—but come at the time you know to be best.

> "Jesus has come to redeem where it is wrong and heal the world where it is broken. His miracles are not just proofs that he has power but also wonderful foretastes of what he is going to do with that power."
>
> **Timothy Keller**

DAY 187

They feast on the abundance of your house;
you give them drink from your river of delights.
For with you is the fountain of life.

PSALM 36:8-9

Everything good, enjoyable, refreshing, fascinating, and interesting derives from our gracious God. People who reject God now can maintain the illusion that life is good without him, only because in his kindness he has not withdrawn all his good gifts.

> "God can't give us peace and happiness apart
> from himself because there is no such thing."
>
> C.S. Lewis

DAY 188

*In him we were also chosen, having
been predestined according to the plan
of him who works out everything in
conformity with the purpose of his will.*

EPHESIANS 1:11

When we read Scripture we're left with the choice to trust—
or not—that God works even in our most difficult circumstances. When we see God as he really is, holy and
loving, just and merciful, full of grace and always thinking
of our eternal good, we can bow to his plans and trust him.
Thomas Brooks said, "A gracious soul may look through
the darkest cloud and see God smiling on him."

> "As sure as ever God puts his children in the
> furnace, he will be in the furnace with them."
>
> **Charles Spurgeon**

DAY 189

This is love: not that we loved God, but
that he loved us and sent his Son as
an atoning sacrifice for our sins.

1 JOHN 4:10

In all human history, who has paid the highest price for evil and suffering? Poll a hundred people on this question, and only a few would come up with the right answer: God. That's the meaning of grace, the significance of the cross. The depths of grace can never be overstated.

> "Christ took upon him our nature, and in that nature suffered hunger and was subject to all infirmities; therefore when we are put to difficulties in our callings, to troubles for a good conscience, or to any hardship in the world, we must labor for contentment, because we are only with hardness made conformable unto Christ; we suffer, then reign with him."
>
> **Richard Sibbes**

DAY 190

How beautiful on the mountains
are the feet of those who bring good news.

ISAIAH 52:7

Peace, safety, and economic prosperity are threatened in the world's crises. The world's main problem is that it's inhabited by people like us, sinners in need of redemption. Thirsty people need us to reach out and extend to them the cold water of Christ's grace. "For he has rescued us from the dominion of darkness and brought us into the kingdom of the Son he loves" (Colossians 1:13).

> "I would sooner bring one sinner to Jesus Christ
> than unravel all the mysteries of the divine Word,
> for salvation is the one thing we are to live for."
>
> **Charles Spurgeon**

DAY 191

*To do what is right and just
is more acceptable to the LORD than sacrifice.
Haughty eyes and a proud heart—
the unplowed field of the wicked—produce sin.*

PROVERBS 21:3-4

Pride is a heavy burden. There's nothing like that feeling of lightness when God graciously lifts our self-illusions from our shoulders. Even refusing to forgive ourselves is an act of pride—it's making ourselves and our sins bigger than God and his grace. Dietrich Bonhoeffer said of the grace of Jesus, "It is costly because it condemns sin, and grace because it justifies the sinner."

> "When people say, 'I know God forgives me, but I can't forgive myself,' they mean that they have failed an idol, whose approval is more important than God's."
>
> Timothy Keller

DAY 192

*My heart leaps for joy
and with my song I praise him.*

PSALM 28:7

We should see God's grace everywhere in his creation: in the food we eat, the friendships we enjoy, and the pleasures of family, work, and hobbies. But we should never let these secondary pleasures eclipse our love for God (in fact, sometimes we must forgo them to serve God more effectively). We should thank him for all of life's joys and allow them to draw us closer to him.

> "Whatsoever we have over-loved, idolized, and leaned upon, God has from time to time broken it, and made us to see the vanity of it; so that we find the readiest course to be rid our comforts is to set our hearts inordinately or immoderately upon them."

John Flavel

DAY 193

Be kind and compassionate to one another, forgiving each other, just as in Christ God forgave you.

Ephesians 4:32

Extending grace frees us from the terrible burden of resentment and bitterness. Anyone's sins against me, bad as they may be, are far less than my sins against God. Once I grasp this, forgiveness of others becomes far easier, and the relief of that forgiveness will flood my life. Grace may seem distant to us until we think of Jesus, the very heart and soul and incarnation of God's grace. Joni Eareckson Tada says, "God doesn't just give us grace; he gives us Jesus, the Lord of grace."

> "Our soul should be a mirror of Christ...for every grace in Christ there should be a counterpart in us."
>
> **Robert Murray M'Cheyne**

DAY 194

And that is what some of you were. But you were washed, you were sanctified, you were justified in the name of the Lord Jesus Christ and by the Spirit of our God.

1 CORINTHIANS 6:11

Until we come to grips with the fact that we're of the same stock as Stalin and Mao, we'll never get over thinking we deserve better. Evil done to us will offend us and having to suffer will outrage us. We'll never appreciate Christ's grace so long as we hold on to the proud illusion we're better than we are.

> "I saw so much of the wickedness of my heart that I longed to get away from myself...I felt almost pressed to death with my own vileness. Oh what a body of death is there in me...Oh the closest walk with God is the sweetest heaven that can be enjoyed on earth!"
>
> **David Brainerd**

DAY 195

Christ was sacrificed once to take away the sins of many; and he will appear a second time, not to bear sin, but to bring salvation to those who are waiting for him.

Hebrews 9:28

We live our lives between the first coming of Christ and the second. We look back to that first Christmas and the life of Jesus on Earth for some thirty-three years—but we look forward to the Christmas in which the resurrected Christ will return and we, his resurrected people, will live with him forever on the New Earth.

"Christmas is about judgment and grace. Jesus was born to bear our judgment so God's grace could be extended to us."

Paul Tripp

DAY 196

Salvation is found in no one else [but Jesus], for there is no other name under heaven given to mankind by which we must be saved.

Acts 4:12

Only when our sins are dealt with in Christ can we enter Heaven. We cannot pay our own way. We must clearly see the difference between what we can do and what our gracious and merciful Jesus already has done. If we get it right about Jesus, we can afford to get it wrong about secondary things. If we get it wrong about Jesus, it doesn't much matter what else we get right.

> "What! Get to heaven on your own strength? Why, you might as well try to climb to the moon on a rope of sand!"
>
> **George Whitefield**

DAY 197

*Serve the LORD with fear
and celebrate his rule with trembling.*

PSALM 2:11

In Narnia, King Tirian said, "Do you think I keep him in my wallet, fools? Who am I that I could make Aslan appear at my bidding? He's not a tame lion."

The undemanding God who exists to serve us is a modern heresy. The God of the Bible, though he came in the form of a Servant, still calls the shots. We are servants of a fierce King, and although he is gracious, he never grants us ultimate control. We need to be reminded that Jesus is God—and we are not!

> "We don't fear God because he's bad.
> We stand in utter awe before him
> because he's so good it's scary."
>
> J. Budziszewski

DAY 198

*So then, each of us will give an
account of ourselves to God.*

Romans 14:12

Augustine said, "Grace is given not because we have done
good works, but in order that we may be able to do them."

When we stand before God, our ability to play foot-
ball, manage a company, or write a book will mean nothing. Our dependence on Christ, to cleanse us of sin and
empower us to a new way of living—grace-filled and fruit-
ful—will mean everything.

Donald Whitney says, "Advance in the Christian life
comes not by the work of the Holy Spirit alone, nor by our
work alone, but by our responding to and cooperating with
the grace the Holy Spirit initiates and sustains."

> "Consider, to provoke you to good
> works, that you shall have from God,
> when you come to glory, a reward for
> everything you do for him on earth."
>
> John Bunyan

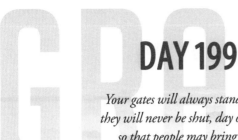

DAY 199

Your gates will always stand open,
they will never be shut, day or night,
so that people may bring you
the wealth of the nations—
their kings led in triumphal procession.

Isaiah 60:11

Heaven's greatest miracle will be our access to God. Think of it! In the New Jerusalem, we will be able to come physically, through wide open gates, to God's throne. We will bring tribute to the King of kings, who is both our Savior and our Friend (John 15:15). Together we'll forever celebrate his boundless grace to us.

> "It was grace which on earth said to us, 'Come unto me, and I will give you rest'; and it will be grace, in all its exceeding riches, that will hereafter say to us, 'Come, you who are blessed of my Father, inherit the kingdom prepared for you from the foundation of the world.'"
>
> **Horatius Bonar**

DAY 200

We have different gifts, according to
the grace given to each of us.

ROMANS 12:6

Father, thank you that our gifts and passions are not an accident but are part of the way you've wired us. Thank you for intricately designing each of us to uniquely express your glory. Surely this will be all the more true on the New Earth, where we'll be forever delivered from everything that hinders our worship. May our work today be enriched and motivated by this destiny you've set before us.

"When I go to the grave I can say, as others have said, 'My day's work is done.' But I cannot say, 'My life is done.' My work will recommence the next morning. The tomb is not a blind alley; it is a thoroughfare. It closes upon the twilight but opens upon the dawn."

Victor Hugo

DAY 201

As the Father has loved me, so have I loved you.
Now remain in my love. If you keep my commands,
you will remain in my love...
I have told you this so that my joy may be in
you and that your joy may be complete.

JOHN 15:9-11

Jesus tells us about God's grace and love toward us so that his joy may be in us and our joy may be full and abiding. Decades later, the apostle John, remembering Jesus's words, said, "We are writing to tell you these things, because this makes us truly happy" (1 John 1:4 CEV). As we speak words of grace and live lives of grace, we enter into God's happiness, which fills us and spills out on those around us.

> "No amount of regret changes the past. No amount of anxiety changes the future. Any amount of grateful joy changes the present."
>
> **Ann Voskamp**

DAY 202

[God] chose us in [Christ] before the creation of the world to be holy and blameless in his sight.

EPHESIANS 1:4

We're accustomed to thinking highly of our God-given choices. We would do well to worshipfully contemplate God graciously choosing us in Christ before the world began, to deliver us from sin and death, and to allow us to live with him in everlasting happiness. What grace!

"There may be love between equals, and an inferior may love a superior; but love in a superior, and so superior as he may do what he will, in such a one love is called grace...Now God, who is an infinite Sovereign, who might have chosen whether ever he would love us or no, for him to love us, this is grace."

Thomas Goodwin

DAY 203

Sing the glory of his name;
make his praise glorious.

PSALM 66:2

Gratitude, thanksgiving, and praise are the natural responses of our hearts when we recognize that ours is a God of grace and that his grace is what the universe is all about. There is no purpose higher than his glory, no attribute greater than grace. "But grow in the grace and knowledge of our Lord and Savior Jesus Christ. To him be glory..." (2 Peter 3:18).

May the amazing grace of Jesus always be the air we breathe!

"When we've been there ten thousand years,
Bright, shining as the sun,
We've no less days to sing God's praise
Than when we first begun."

John Newton

CONCLUSION

Recognizing Our Need for God's Daily Grace

In 1987, eighteen-month-old "Baby Jessica" fell twenty-two feet into a Texas well. Rescuers labored nonstop to save her. After fifty-five grueling hours, her life hanging in the balance, they finally extracted her from the well. The nation breathed a sigh of relief and cheered the heroes.

Note that what happened was *not* this: "Baby Jessica clawed her eighteen-month-old body up the side of that twenty-two-foot well, inch by inch, digging in her little toes and working her way up. She's a hero, that Jessica!"

Baby Jessica was utterly helpless. Her fate was in the hands of her rescuers. Left to herself, Jessica had no chance. When it comes to our salvation, we're utterly helpless too. That's grace: "At just the right time, when we were still powerless, Christ died for the ungodly" (Romans 5:6).

We get no more applause for our redemption than Baby Jessica got for being rescued. God alone deserves the ovation. He's the only hero. And it didn't just cost him fifty-five hours of hard work—it cost him everything.

"Who has ever given to God, that God should repay them?" (Romans 11:35). The answer is *no one.*

We deserved expulsion; he gives us a diploma. We deserved the electric chair; he gives us a parade. Anything less than overwhelming gratitude should be unthinkable. (Why not stop and thank him now?)

Many believers live in spiritual poverty, oblivious to the riches they possess in Christ. God calls us to continue to acknowledge our spiritual impotence, *accept his everyday grace*, and live in heartfelt gratitude.

We don't need to look under rocks to find grace. Philip Yancey says, "Grace is everywhere, like lenses that go unnoticed because you are looking through them."

Yet at the very center of grace, at the center of the universe itself, is the person and work of Christ. If you have not yet cried out to God and confessed your sins and placed your faith in Jesus, you can do so, by his grace, right now. Nothing could be more important!

Perhaps you feel you've wasted your life or squandered your opportunities to turn to God. Well, maybe you have, but François Mauriac says, "That is the mystery of grace: it never comes too late." If you are reading this, it's not too late to embrace the redemptive grace of Jesus.

As for those who already know Jesus, D.L. Moody put it

well: "A man can no more take in a supply of grace for the future than he can eat enough for the next six months, or take sufficient air into his lungs at one time to sustain life for a week. We must draw upon God's boundless store of grace from day to day, as we need it."

C.S. Lewis wrote in *The Four Loves*, "Grace substitutes a full, childlike and delighted acceptance of our need, a joy in total dependence. We become 'jolly beggars.'" Not pathetic beggars, but *jolly* ones!

True grace undercuts not only self-righteousness but self-sufficiency. "Let us then *approach God's throne of grace with confidence*" (Hebrews 4:16, emphasis added). Because of Christ's work, God's door is always open, his supply of grace always overflowing.

May we remember each day just how desperately we need the grace of Jesus. Because of his freely given grace, we have every reason for gratitude and happiness.

WHAT NEXT?

All Christ-centered, biblically based treatments of the subject of grace lend themselves to repeated reflection. You may wish to reread this book and meditate on or memorize the Scripture at its core.

Here are some other books on God's grace that you may find helpful:

- *Transforming Grace*, Jerry Bridges
- *Grace: More Than We Deserve, Greater Than We Imagine*, Max Lucado
- *What's So Amazing About Grace?*, Philip Yancey
- *Future Grace*, John Piper
- *The Grace Awakening*, Charles Swindoll
- *The Grace and Truth Paradox*, Randy Alcorn

Scripture Quotation Sources

Unless otherwise indicated, Scripture quotations are from the Holy Bible, New International Version®, NIV®. Copyright © 1973, 1978, 1984, 2011 by Biblica, Inc.® Used by permission. All rights reserved worldwide.

Verses marked NLT are taken from the *Holy Bible*, New Living Translation. Copyright © 1996, 2004, 2007, 2013 by Tyndale House Foundation. Used by permission of Tyndale House Publishers, Inc., Carol Stream, Illinois 60188. All rights reserved.

Verses marked NASB are taken from the New American Standard Bible®, © 1960, 1962, 1963, 1968, 1971, 1972, 1973, 1975, 1977, 1995 by The Lockman Foundation. Used by permission. (www.Lockman.org)

Verses marked CEV are taken from the Contemporary English Version © 1991, 1992, 1995 by American Bible Society, Used by permission.

Verses marked GNT are taken from the Good News Translation in Today's English Version—Second Edition. Copyright © 1992 by American Bible Society. Used by permission.

About the Author

Randy Alcorn is the founder and director of Eternal Perspective Ministries and a *New York Times* best-selling author of fifty books, including *Heaven* (over one million sold), *The Treasure Principle* (over two million sold), *If God Is Good*, *Happiness*, and the award-winning novel *Safely Home*. His books sold exceed nine million copies and have been translated into about seventy languages.

Alcorn resides in Gresham, Oregon, with his wife, Nanci. They have two married daughters and five grandsons. Randy enjoys hanging out with his family, biking, underwater photography, research, and reading.

Contact Eternal Perspective Ministries at www.epm.org or 39085 Pioneer Blvd., Suite 206, Sandy, OR 97055 or 503.668.5200. Follow Randy on Facebook: www.facebook.com/randyalcorn; Twitter: www.twitter.com/randyalcorn; and on his blog: www.epm.org/blog.

To learn more about Harvest House books and
to read sample chapters, visit our website:

www.harvesthousepublishers.com

HARVEST HOUSE PUBLISHERS
EUGENE, OREGON